The Kids of Wildflower Hill

by

June Rose

Table of Contents

Foreword

Twelve years passed between the start of this book and its completion. I didn't set out to write a book, but just to record the delightful experiences I was having with my beloved animals. These I would share with friends in Christmas letters, usually accompanying the text with small drawings of my "kids." When I saw the volume of notes I had collected, I realized it could become a book.

Through the years of writing these letters and the book, my understanding of my animal friends changed dramatically. In the beginning I had seen them as simple-minded creatures that delighted me with their antics, and communication was very limited. However, I soon came to perceive in my animals the full range of emotions that I had always thought belonged exclusively to human beings. It was a real awakening. I have seen in them, joy, anger, hate, fear, both emotional and physical pain, jealousy, sympathy, compassion, grief, loneliness, and most abundantly love. Animals don't hide their feelings; they are always honest and up front. This book includes examples of their unique expressions of all these emotions.

I had made many discoveries about the nature of animals through my personal experiences, but it wasn't until around the tenth year at Wildflower Hill that I truly understood. I came across three remarkable women who are able to connect with the minds of animals and share their wisdom with us.

Just before Samantha Josephine, our wonderful golden retriever, died, I happened on a book that helped me through her dying process, and eased the pain. In her book, *Blessing the Bridge: A Spiritual Guide to Helping an Animal Die in Peace and Dignity*, Rita Reynolds talks of finding herself creating a hospice for creatures about to transition. She records these rich experiences in the book, greatly helping owners grieving over the loss of a beloved pet.

My animals taught me a new perspective on death and dying. For them it is a natural progression of life that they accept so peacefully. I believe they understand that death is transition to another world, instead of oblivion.

Sonya Fitzpatrick became well known as the Pet Psychic through her TV show. Her interaction with animals, on camera, brought me a whole new dimension in relations between animals and people. No longer do I doubt that animals understand what we say.

The experience that I most identified with concerned a miniature horse which had stopped eating. Her desperate owners took her to several vets. No one could tell them why she wouldn't eat. There was no physical reason. The mare told Sonya that she was grieving because her baby had been taken from her before she had completed her responsibilities as a mother. The shocked owners acknowledged that she had been very distressed as she watched them load her foal into a trailer and take it away. The little mare asked if she could have another baby and if it, too, would be taken. Her owners then apologized to the mare and told her that, if she would start eating, she could have another foal, and they also agreed they would wait until that baby was older, and promised they would alert her in advance of taking it away. Immediately after the discussion, the little mare started eating again. This was only one of countless incidents I watched that confirmed for me that we can communicate with animals.

In practicing what I learned from watching Sonya's show I gained a new perspective that helped me to work with my animals, and to comfort them in times of stress. I am careful of what I say around them, as I know they are listening and understand.

I found it very touching that the most frequently asked question by the animals Sonya talks with is, "Will my owner be keeping me?" This seems to worry them greatly.

Amelia Kinkade was another pet psychic who has profoundly affected my understanding of animals. In her book, *Straight from the Horse's Mouth*, she relates many more experiences similar to those of Sonya's. She tells an incredible story of the search for a cat which had disappeared. Amelia was able to communicate with the cat who could only tell them she was in a dark place and that she had no food or water. Amelia and the owner searched the neighborhood thoroughly, looking in cellars and dark places, finding no cat. After about a week of continuing communication and stress, the owner received a call from a couple on a motor trip who had just opened their luggage to find the cat. The cat, very hungry and thirsty, was saved. In her book Amelia strives to teach the reader how they, too, can learn to communicate psychically with animals, as she does.

As I write this we are having a welcome snowfall. Outside I see my Australian shepherd, Dakota, ecstatically cavorting, dancing in circles, catching the flakes, pouncing on his ball, half hidden in the snow, just like wolves I've seen hunting mice. He licks the snow, then races full tilt around the entire house. It gladdens my heart to watch him; scenes like this continually brought joy and delight into my life.

The intent of this book is to create a greater understanding of our animal friends and their lives. Animals have all the emotions that we humans experience, and they, too, feel life deeply. They understand what we say and our emotions, and we humans need to treat them with greater respect and lavish them with all the love and attention they crave from us.

I share many deaths herein, but death is an important part of the living experience that animals seem to understand better than humans. I believe they instinctively know that death is a transition point, not an end, and do not fear it. It was often heartbreaking for me to know I would no longer have their blessed presence, but I had no choice in the matter.

I find it amazing that animals know to read you by looking into your face at eyes. The chickens who feared me would particularly avoid me when I looked at them, and when I wasn't looking at them, they were fearless and often got under my feet, while the hens I was on intimate terms with would communicate by looking me directly in the eye, "eye to eye." Horse whisperer, Monty Roberts, uses eye contact in training horses who can find a look intimidating and even threatening. The leader of a wild horse herd, usually the alpha mare, controls her clan, even young stallions, by her eye.

Dealing with animals should always be an exercise in love, and very importantly, my animals have truly taught me about love. My capacity for love grew immensely through our relationships. They taught me that the more love you feel, the more love you have, the more love you give away, the more love comes back to you. Love helped me to weather many difficult times in those years, and I am a far better person than the woman who first moved to Wildflower Hill.

I am deeply grateful to my beloved animal "kids," for all they continued to teach me. They have enriched my life more than I could ever have imagined. May we always be blessed by our beloved animals.

Wildflower Hill

The moment I saw the picture in the Prescott Real Estate Guide, I knew this would be our place. A long drive lined with split rail fencing, backed with cottonwoods and pine trees, led up to the cozy farmhouse on two-and-a-half acres. The advertisement mentioned fruit trees and a guest apartment above the garage, a small barn which included two chicken roosting/nesting rooms, a feed/storage and tack room, and corrals; perfect for us. This was to be our new home, and I knew before we even saw it.

The living room/dining room was paneled in wood with a high beamed ceiling, and windows all around bringing in wonderful views of prairie extending to distant purple mountains. A wide deck served three sides of the home, with one side enclosed as a screened porch. In a corner of the living room sat a wood stove which provided cozy warmth on cold winter days.

The studio apartment over the garage was perfect for my needs. It, too, had large windows on all four sides. Since it was on the second floor it afforded incredible views, including nearby Granite Mountain. From my desk I could watch the oncoming weather, sweeping over the mountain bringing winter snows or summer rains. There was a small deck from which I loved to watch the rising of the full moon on warm summer nights. I recall one afternoon watching a storm coming up from the south where there was lightning from dark clouds. I could see a rainbow following thinner clouds, and in the west the sky was clear as I watched the golden setting sun. How magnificent it was to have these sweeping views that could expand and clear the mind and heart.

My friend Earl and I had each always lived in large cities, but now in our semi-retirement years we decided we wanted some land on which to grow our own food, and surround ourselves with a variety of wonderful animals. I had always loved animals, but never had any of my own. Most of my life had been devoted to pursuing an assortment of careers ranging from a fashion designer in New York, a TV commercial producer, and as an advertising executive in Phoenix. Earl, on the other hand, had enjoyed life as a successful architect in Southern California. We met after we had both moved to Phoenix.

The house had two bedrooms and since Earl was the single parent of an eleven year old son, E.J., they took over the house while I had the garage apartment and my own private space. In the evenings I preferred reading and watching PBS shows, leaving them to enjoy sitcoms and action movies in the house.

The previous owners of the property, feeling the area had become too crowded, had bought a place with more land and wide open space in the northwest. They assured us that the chickens would move to a new home before we took possession. Since we planned to have chickens, I wrote into the contract that the sale was contingent upon the chickens staying. They stayed, and from the first day we enjoyed wonderful eggs.

Even before we closed on the property, over a chilly January weekend, we bought 15 more fruit trees, dug the holes and planted them. The trees matured and blessed us with many years of luscious cherries, peaches, apricots, plums, nectarines, pears and apples. In addition to lots of gardening time, I spent much of the summer drying, canning and freezing fruit to enjoy over the winter.

Vegetables and herbs supported us all year with herbs for cooking and healing. Even after a summer of bounty, I discovered that with a protective mulch blanket I could harvest potatoes, beets, carrots, Jerusalem artichokes and onions all winter as needed, and arugula, my amazing salad green, was winter hardy. Each winter night, it froze solid as an icicle, then thawed as the sun warmed the earth. We built a small greenhouse where I grew broccoli, lettuce, leeks and chard from fall until spring.

The first spring was glorious. All the fruit trees burst into bloom and the ground was covered with wildflowers. There were charming little ones that grew about three inches high, each single stem holding a three inch wide, white flower. There were poppies, Mexican Hats, Indian Paintbrushes, wild Zinnias and more. That was when I decided to call our new home Wildflower Hill.

Neither Earl nor I had ever lived on a farm. Nothing in our backgrounds had prepared us to be farmers. It was a new experience, mostly learned the hard way. Sometimes that's the best, as you find new ways to do things because no one told you it wouldn't work. I was proud of the creative solutions I came up with, such as letting some crops go to seed and plant themselves, and after the first year I didn't have to sow seeds of carrots, beets, onions, leeks or arugula. In going to seed they produced carpets of plants that I only had to thin out, transplant, or give to new homes.

We pretty much created a self-sustaining microcosm. Water from our well supplied our needs, as well as the plants that fed and nourished us, our animals and the wild birds. The horses and chickens produced manure to feed the plants. If it became necessary, we could cut trees to supply the energy needed to cook and heat. A generator filled in at those times when the power grid shut off our electricity.

It was a joy to greet the day. Each morning I'd open the door to be met by the dogs, Marshall Goodboy right there with his wagging tail, and Samantha Josephine excitedly dancing in circles. On our way to the barn, the two of them energetically engaged in their ritual of mock aggression. Near the chicken yard, the hens would spot me and come racing, with wing assist, to the fence corner, while the horses whinny their "good mornings;" a very welcoming start to any day.

The farm was constantly changing. Annually, we endured the scourge of grasshoppers, blister beetles and gophers, weather traumas, animals dying and new ones arriving. Some years brought bumper crops and others small harvests, although one thing that never changed was the workload; but our air was always clean. What a joy to step into the garden to pick fresh foods for our table and our animals, organic food with wonderful flavor and nourishment for our bodies. I loved being able to give my beloved animals an ideal home. To live without this joy and abundance became unimaginable.

The Chicks

Many years before we moved to Wildflower Hill, I had a sophisticated friend who raised chickens. I remember wondering how a cultivated, intelligent, worldly man could be interested in chickens. It just didn't compute with my image of him. Now, I too, a cultivated, intelligent, sophisticated woman, find chickens absolutely delightful. For one thing they have exquisitely beautiful plumage, with all those intricate colors and patterns designed by the Master. Aracanas look like pheasants in a wonderful combination of autumn tones from rusts through many shades of brown with a touch of black, and tufts of feathers on their cheeks like mutton-chop whiskers. Silver Wyandots have black and white streaked headdresses cascading over feathers that look like silver petals outlined in black with a black center vein. White leghorns remind me of lovely angels. Only angels could maintain such pristine white feathers. Then there are the Rhode Island reds in rust, and the barred rocks in gray and white stripes.

Each year, when buying chicks, I'd try for a variety of breeds, just to revel in the beauty of their plumage. Newborn chicks generally come in yellow or brown. Slowly their feathers emerge, and in six months they display incredibly beautiful raiment. Ravena was a lustrous, coal black, like a raven. Dalmatia was a petite, white girl with black spots. Lucille (Ball) was a gorgeous Rhode Island Red, of course.

The birds reminded me of ballerinas. I would often see them point a toe, slowly step forward onto it, lift the other leg and pose for a bit before moving on, graceful and elegant. Just under the tail, each hen carries a beautiful cluster of feathers that form what looks like a peony flower. Tipping forward to peck the ground they'd expose fluffy down bottoms, and I was reminded of my completely feminine sister, Victoria. When she was a baby Vicky insisted on wearing her panties backward so that the frilly bottoms showed to the front. Chickens have eyes on the sides of their heads and look at you in profile. When viewed head on you can barely see their eyes, so I've always wondered how can a hen peck a seed the size of a pinhead from a collection of rock and dirt on the ground directly in front of her?

Chicken society is class conscious and hierarchical – you've heard of the "pecking order." At the top are the senior hens, the old gals. Based on their year of birth, the ranking descends. The rooster is not "top dog." He floats somewhere in the middle in his role to defend the flock and fertilize eggs. Hens of the same breed hang out together in cliques; must give them a sense of family. Even as babies they sort themselves by breed and color. A one-of-a-kind hen is often on the fringe by herself. A strange hen has to earn the right to socialize with the others, and is accepted very slowly.

Even though a batch of chicks is sold as pullets (females), there's no guarantee all will be hens. We never knew how many chicks would become roosters until we heard this funny "uh–uh–uh–uuhhh" early in the morning. It must have been embarrassing to them to make such a silly sound, but they always persisted until they achieved a respectable full-bodied crow about the time they reached sexual maturity.

One year I ended up with three males, which we didn't want, as we already had two roosters. Too many roosters mean cock fights. I happened to meet a commercial breeder in the supermarket who mentioned he needed a rooster. I asked if he'd trade one of his hens for a beautiful, young Aracana rooster. He brought me Rosie, a breed unknown to me, only available to big poultry growers. I named her Rosie when she started laying eggs with a pinkish tint.

The tip of a chick's beak is commonly cut off by commercial breeders to prevent these poor hens who live jammed together in small cages from pecking each other to death. Rosie, a butterscotch colored beauty with a snub nose, was very frightened, missing the hens she knew and moving to a strange environment. Our chicken yard/ horse corral was the size of the average city lot. Holding Rosie close I carried her about, showing her where to find feed and water, telling the other hens that she was now part of the family. When I put her down she immediately ran back into the empty chicken house to hide. That night I checked and found her trying to roost on a salt block in the horse shelter. I picked her up, carried her into the hen house and gently tucked her into a corner. That became her corner, and that's where she slept until the others accepted her and permitted her to roost with them.

After this TLC, Rosie came to think of me as mom. Every time I went into the chicken yard, she'd greet me with a special sound – a cross between "poh, poh, poh" and a coo.

I'd mimic the sound, which I learned is reassuring to all chickens. In the morning

I'd throw scratch to the hens, and as soon as I entered the yard there was Rosie asking for hers from my hand. What dropped on the ground was for the other hens to pick up. Whenever I called her name, Rosie came running, expecting a treat, which she always got. Standing on her tippy toes, she'll look me directly in the eye in anticipation. Eating quickly, she'd stop ever so often to cock an eye out for any competition. When she gulped too fast the food jammed up in her throat, causing her to cough with a funny little squeak. After she finished, she'd stroll off, leaving me with a soft coo, which I took as "thank you."

The day I painted the chicken house, Rosie was right there watching everything I did, checking the paint pan and bucket, examining the ladder. When Earl and I built a new shelter for my horse, Keebe, Rosie scrutinized the whole process. Since we had no others of her breed, she was a loner who entertained herself exploring the yard. As my favorite she received preferential treatment. Having a friend in high places gave her rank and confidence. After a while, she didn't need me as much and I felt like my child had graduated to a new independence. Rosie became accepted, and a happy hen of higher standing.

I came to learn some of the language of chickens. In contentment they toot softly. A rolling gorgle seems to mean things are almost satisfactory, "Hey, I'm doing O.K. right now, but don't bug me." Hens quickly fly into hysteria if you try to rush them, but will cooperate if you move slowly and make reassuring sounds. If I needed to pick up an injured hen or catch one that had gotten out of the yard, I found I could calm her by imitating the "poh, poh, poh" voice that hens use to communicate with each other. If the voice is high, the hen is usually happy. When the voice drops it's usually a sign of irritation or annoyance.

It is important for a hen to select the right spot for the night. The oldest usually wander into the hen house well before dusk to get their roosting spots, while the young kids stay out until almost dark. If a senior hen wants the spot claimed by a lesser hen she will displace her, which then causes a chain reaction down the pecking order. The whole house can be upset as a flapping, squawking game of musical chairs takes place. Ten minutes can pass before everyone is finally set. After selecting the right spot, a hen will grip the roosting pole firmly, settle her body, drop head and tail in an effort to curl around the pole, then slip into a sound sleep. They aren't easily disturbed until dawn and their rooster wake-up call.

One evening I watched in fascination as Rosie, last into the hen house, tried to find a place for the night. She entered the room and stretched tall to see if the nesting box was occupied. It was. She walked along under the roosting poles looking up for a place. Only narrow spaces between the roosting hens were left. Rosie made a couple of attempts to jump onto one of those spots, but didn't make it. She went back to check the nesting box again. Next, she checked a spot on the floor by the door. That didn't suit her, so she ran out the door, around outside to the other hen room, where she repeated the same routine. Then back to the first room and the whole game began again. All of this to the accompaniment of much squawking and flapping of wings by the hens that were annoyed by the disruption. About dark, the scenario ended as Rosie settled for space on the floor with the "tubbie babies," Cornish game chicks who had become too heavy to fly up to roosting poles.

These fast growing birds usually go to market in eight weeks... a very brief lifetime. I had purchased three of them, and one Turken, who I named Tallulah. Although a Turken is a chicken, with its bare neck it looks like a small turkey. The Cornish chicks had huge legs and feet, and their bodies grew fast and heavy for their legs. At night they huddled with Tallulah in the straw under the roosting hens above.

The Cornish kids were a delight. I called them my tubbie babies after the Teletubbies from the children's TV show. I could almost see them grow bigger and fatter each day. It made me laugh to see these fat kids in a fast waddle as they tried to catch grasshoppers. Their enormous weight became burdensome and awkward, and they would frequently plop down and pant, instead of strolling about like the other chickens. Eight weeks came and went. At four months they had grown well past the age man had designed them for. They could hardly walk and seldom did, even sitting in front of their feeding bowls to eat. Life was a burden. It was time to end their stress. I did so reluctantly, and they ended up in our freezer.

Sunny days were perfect for dust bathing. There was always a previously dug chicken-sized basin in the soft dirt. A hen would lie on her side and scratch dirt up and over her body as she rustled her feathers to distribute it. It's a way to control mites.

Next she'd contort her body to dust her head and neck, too. The routine was then repeated on the other side.

Hens love to play in the mud. When I drained the horse trough they'd all come running, sloshing around in the mud, drinking the water and pecking up bits of who knows what. I've even seen them abandon food to play in the water.

If chickens don't get enough protein and calcium they may eat eggs. By nature, they are used to eating grubs, bugs, caterpillars and such, even lizards. In the summer I'd find plenty of these snacks, which I collected as I gardened. I'd call and the chickens would come running, hopping, flying and flapping, to get their handouts.

Frequently, I had to tolerate a hen eating eggs because I was never sure who is doing the eating, and besides, they lay more than they eat. But when they did eat, they'd splatter the yolk on the other eggs. Dried yolk is hard to clean off the egg shells. Poultry raisers say that you should kill a hen as soon as she starts eating eggs, but that was hard for me to do. However, at one point it became quite a problem, and I knew who was eating eggs. It was Mantilla. I spoke to her and told her she would be done in if she didn't stop. For a while things got better. Then she started eating eggs again. What to do? At the time I had five young hens in a separate yard. I could put Mantilla in with them, as they were not laying yet.

She was hard to catch, and since she had understood my threat, she was on her guard against me. One night I snatched her off the roost as she was sleeping. To prevent her from flying over the fence back to the flock, I clipped the feathers of one wing and put her in with the younger ones, but that didn't do it. In the morning, she was back with the flock. Next evening I clipped the other wing. After a third clipping, she had to stay put. I told her if she didn't, the next step was to cut off her head. Mantilla became quite angry with me for not letting her back with her friends. Every time she saw me she let me know how upset she was, and a low harsh "caw" would emerge from her throat as she glared at me. When the young ones joined the older hens, Mantilla went too, but she no longer ate eggs.

However, a year later, Mantilla started eating eggs again and I feared the other hens would pick up this bad habit from her. As she was now an older hen of about seven, I decided I had to do her in. I thanked her for all the eggs she had given us and told her I was releasing her to heaven. One whack with the ax and it was over; she did not suffer. I did not want her to be wasted so she became a wonderful pot of stock. Earl would never eat one of our girls, so the meat always went to the dogs. I thought she might be too old to still be laying, so I was quite surprised to find in her body, one egg with a shell that would have been laid that day, as well as five yolks in different stages of development ranging in size from one-quarter inch to almost full size. I decided that even old hens could still lay, though less frequently, and I would never sacrifice another, instead let them die from old age.

My chickens were an ongoing source of delight, and I hoped there could always be chickens in my life.

Pud 'n Min

Within a week of moving to Wildflower Hill, Earl's eleven-year-old son E.J. asked for a kitten – specifically a black one. The name he chose was Natas. It seemed a strange name. Only later did he tell us it was "Satan" spelled backwards. I know kids can be fascinated by the dark side, but I had a problem with the name and decided to call him Puddie Pie, which suited him perfectly. Pud was always polite, well mannered and talked a lot. He grew into a handsome shorthaired cat, tall and slim with an exceptionally long tail. Of course, being a cat, he was very independent.

Puddie and E.J. would play hide and seek around the house on cold winter days. He slept on Earl's bed and when Earl got up in the middle of the night to go to the bathroom Pud would always accompany him. Like many cats, he loved to climb into open boxes and dresser drawers. Most of the day he spent outside roaming our territory, catching the few mice he found in the barn. In the evening he and Earl often played a game Earl called Tail. As he lay next to Earl on the couch, Puddie would take the tip of his tail and quickly tap the back of Earl's hand. Earl soon got the message that he was supposed to try and grab it. It was a game that Earl never won, but it was fun for both.

Earl had an airplane and once a year he would fly to Napa Valley for an annual Fourth of July bash held by old friends at their winery. The friends were feeding families of feral cats, who, of course, always had litters of kittens – wild, undisciplined ones. His friends persuaded Earl to take one of them, another black one, back to Arizona. In the plane the kitten escaped its box. In a state of hysteria it flew all over the cabin, pooping everywhere. Quite a mess. Fortunately, I didn't have to do clean-up.

 I named her Menehuni Mittens. A menehuni is a Hawaiian spirit, as she was quite spooky and frowned a lot. She'd put her eyes at half mast and pull her ears out tensely out to the side. I added Mittens because she had extra toes and she had the habit of holding her paws in the air like a child wearing mittens.

Humans were foreign to Min, as we called her, and she had a hard time adjusting to a house. Full of fear, eyes wide, she hid a lot. Often as I watched TV, I would grab her, hold her close and stroke her gently. After a while she decided she liked the touching and, on her own, would join me on the couch, stretching her body along the crack between my arm and the back of the couch. We had bonded. From that point on Min was my cat.

I liked to call her Mini Mu, and she would spend the evening with me until about ten o'clock when we retired. Her place was on the bed with me, nestling in against the crook of my knees or the small of my back. It never seemed to disturb her when I moved or changed positions; she adjusted quickly.

Min didn't grow nearly as large as Puddie. I loved her small, teenager size, like having a perpetual kitten, so light and easy to carry. She, too, had short black fur, but with a tiny white star on her chest. She seldom spoke, and when she did she produced only a soft squeak. A full meow was a sign of great distress.

Min had amazing powers of concentration. We frequently watched animal shows on PBS. Since there were no commercials, the shows were non-stop for an hour. Feline and bird shows were her favorites. She could sit in front of the TV, her face tilted up, riveted to the screen for the full hour. If a bird flew out of the picture, she would get up, check the back of the TV to see where it had gone, in case she could catch it.

When I gardened, Min liked to join me by lying in the catnip bush or under the asparagus fern, a shady place from which to observe the world, and I delighted in her company. On summer afternoons she would recline in an empty flower box attached to the deck rail. The box exactly fit her body, and from there she could watch the last golden rays of the day, as I completed watering the garden.

Our last night together I will never forget. I happened to glance down and saw Min lying on her back, four paws in the air, her upside-down face turned to mine, staring at me intently for a long time. In retrospect, I think she was saying goodbye. I let her out for a quick potty break before hitting the sack. When I called she didn't come, and she wasn't there in the morning. I never saw her again. Puddie Pie had gone a year before. We never knew what happened to either. In our area when small animals disappear, the coyotes are usually to blame.

A couple of years later, one evening as I was driving about a mile from home my headlights picked up small black cat running across the road into a field. Could it be Min? I turned around, drove back to the spot and called, "Min!" The cat came bounding through the grass to me. My heart skipped. It looked like Min, except for the missing star and extra toes. It was not Min.

Even years after their disappearances I still miss Menehuni Mittens and Puddie Pie. Our time with them was just too short. Since so many birds had chosen Wildflower Hill as a haven, a place to nest and raise their families, we decided not to get another cat, until four years later when Charles arrived.

Marshall and Sam

Samantha Josephine and Marshall Goodboy, the dogs at Wildflower Hill, both arrived as puppies, never knowing another real home. Marshall was all boy, non-stop energy, boundless, wagging enthusiasm with an insatiable appetite for love and attention. Sammy Jo, a golden retriever mix, was all female, a sensitive, sweet, gentle lady.

When Sam was a puppy she liked to bark. One day she started barking and Earl told her "no barking." She looked at him and barked again, only not quite as loud. He reprimanded her. She glanced at him and barked more softly. Again, he repeated a little stronger, "no barking!" She studied him, and then slowly opened her mouth without a sound, waiting for his response, peeking at him from the corner of her eye. Just like any young child, she was testing the boundaries.

A year after Sam arrived, Earl wanted to find Labrador retriever, and that's when he brought home a small, round, golden Lab puppy, an adorable baby we named Marshall Goodboy. A roly-poly yellow ball with four legs, on more than one occasion he lost his balance and rolled down the front steps. He didn't bark until he was half grown, but instead would open his mouth and emit a yawning noise, but when he finally did bark it was an enormous sound worthy of a dog twice his size.

Both of Marshall's parents had been skinny chocolate Labs with narrow heads. I prefer the heavier Labs with larger heads and told Marshall that was the way I wanted him to be. And he became a heavy dog with a large head, attributed in part, I feel, to our taking him out with us as we rode the range on horseback. When we started these riding treks I felt Marshall was too young, but Earl insisted he would do just fine, and he did. Running over the grassy hills strengthened his little legs and expanded his heart and lungs. For Sam and him, this was the very best of times. They would race ahead, exploring under bushes, sniffing in gopher holes and trying to catch the pronghorn antelope we often saw. Since these animals are the fastest on the North American continent, I didn't fear for their safety.

Dogs need to feel they have a purpose in life, a role in the family. Sam chose to make our property safe from ravens during the day, and to patrol for intruders during the night. We had many ravens, and Sam, eyes up, would chase them across the sky. When one would land in the top of a cottonwood tree she always let it know this was her territory. At sunset I would see her, head lowered, checking the property, trotting around, just inside the fence line. Sometimes at night I could hear her barking in a far corner of the property and from her voice I knew she was letting the world know she was on the job. So seriously did she take her duties that we saw her on many a cold winter night curled up in the snow instead of her cozy doghouse.

For her first five years Sam would kill any chicken that happened over or under the fence of the chicken yard. She was always severely reprimanded, but continued the killing. It was hard not to laugh the morning she sheepishly brought me her latest kill, instead of letting me find it as I invariably did. I considered getting rid of her, but Earl said Sam could kill every chicken we had before he would give her away.

Finally, I realized that I had been the cause of the problem. In the beginning Earl and I would chase down the hens that got out. We had unwittingly taught Sam that chickens were to be chased and grabbed. She must have believed she was helping us. I tried a new tactic. I would walk up slowly to the escapee, making calming, cooing sounds and pick up the hen. The whole time the stalk was on I would say firmly to the watching Sam, "No chicken!" When I had the hen in my arms I would stroke her and speak in a reassuring tone, the way you do to someone you care about. Sam got the message. There were no more kills.

Sammy Jo was her most creative with her voice. At night she might give forth with a howling session reminiscent of a wolf, but with a twist. At first her lovely voice would ascent to a high point, then slowly descend, going from clarity to the raspy, cracking voice of a crone. After a cluster of yips like a pack of puppies, she would lapse into an assortment of soft uncanine-like sounds, as if she were having an intimate conversation with herself. Marshall would accompany her, but his was just your everyday howl. He couldn't match her nuances and vocal virtuosity, but he tried. I always ended up laughing.

Usually we rode out to a stock tank presided over by a huge, creaking windmill with blades that spanned 12 feet. First thing the dogs would do was jump into the tank and swim around, smiling, lapping the water and wagging tails, which splashed the water

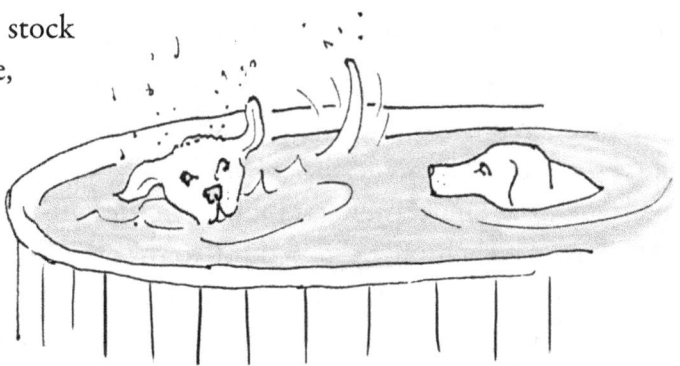

about. Along the way home the dogs would drop into any mud puddle we came across. The quickest way for a dog to cool its body is in water or, if no water is available, to press its tummy to cool earth.

As our area grew, more homes were built. The dirt road in front of Wildflower Hill was widened and paved. The ranch we rode on was still open land, but a new fence was put up without a gate, so our days of riding the open range came to an end.

While watching a TV show about wolves, I noticed a great similarity between wolves and Sam. She had many of the same gestures and postures; the funny little challenge to play, a quick jerk to attention with stiff body and pricked ears. Roughhousing with Marshall, she never demonstrated any intent to harm. I knew she wasn't serious because she'd have a smile on her face and a wagging tail. She would drop on her elbows and bark a fierce-sounding challenge. Feigning ferocity, she would go for Marshall's throat or grab him by a hamstring, like a wolf with wild prey. Or, she might grab his collar and pull him around. Even though I knew Marshall found the game boring, he would usually go along. Had she been serious, he could have taken her down in a flash. Sam was really a sugar cookie and habitually turned tail when seriously challenged. Wolves are family oriented canines, and so was Sam. In contrast, Marshall bore none of the predator wolf traits.

Sam had a funny habit of putting her face into my knees from behind as we walked, almost knocking me off balance. I supposed to her it felt like a special kind of stroking.

Jake, the golden retriever next door, and Sam both had the same trait of coming up from behind and jamming their head between your knees as you stand in conversation with someone.

Marshall's insatiable need for love and attention could drive me to the point of exasperation. His purpose in life was to retrieve things – balls, pinecones, sticks – and he wished to fulfill this destiny whenever he saw anyone. Since I got tired of picking up balls to throw, I quickly taught him to put the ball in my hand. Any guest who came by was immediately brought something to throw. When I worked in the garden I could depend on him to be following my every step with an object to throw. He knew I was occupied with my work and would approach tentatively before dropping a pinecone in the hole I'd just dug. Invariably when he got a loud "NO" he would turn, walk away, sit a moment before returning for a second try. Again he'd come up slowly, watching me out of the corner of his eye, to check me out, then gently lay a toy at my feet. I couldn't help laughing and would usually give in.

Seldom did we have a ball around the place. Balls would never last more than a couple of days, because Marshall would tear them apart as quickly as he could. Since he believed that once a ball, always a ball, he would bring the pieces to be thrown. Incredible as it may seem, you can still actually sail a 4"x4" piece of beach ball for some distance. One moonless night as I came out on the deck to enjoy the stars, he brought me a 1"x 1" piece of tennis ball. I threw it into the inky black, and he actually found and brought it back. Labs have great noses, and I'm certain that he found those little pieces of ball in the dark by smelling them. He never gave up. Whenever I got tired of playing, I would pretend to throw the toy in one direction, then toss it into a bush as Marshall charged off in the other direction. But he would persist until he found it. Another trick I used, if he didn't heed my emphatic "No," was to place the throw object up in a tree. I had seen him sit for hours waiting for it to fall to the ground.

With an ongoing shortage of balls, pinecones became Marshall's throw of choice. Pine trees were in abundance in our area so I often used them to mulch the fruit trees. Pine trees come with pinecones, so Marshall had a ready supply. As with balls, he chewed up these stiff, prickly cones. They had to be rather painful on the gums, but they did a great job of cleaning his teeth.

Marshall was the undisputed King of Fetch. Sam knew better than to compete with him, however, she would take any opportunity to steal his toy and taunt him. She took great delight in his frustration. He never tried to get a ball from her, but would cry for us to get it for him. One day she got his ball. Sitting on the deck at the top of the steps with her eyes on him, she nudged the ball gently forward. Marsh whined and looked at me for permission to grab it. Sam pushed the ball out a bit more and down one step. Marshall leapt forward, Sam snatched it up, raised it high as a warrior would a trophy and strode off waving her tail.

Sam would never play fetch with us, but often played ball with herself. Picking up the ball in her mouth she'd throw it in the air, sometimes catching it, sometimes pouncing on it, and throwing it up again, entertaining herself for quite a while.

The difference between the sexes was most pronounced at mealtime. Marshall, all boy, was rambunctious, energetic, and jumping. Right there at the feeding station, he'd be whining. Marshall got to lick the spoon after the canned meat was dished over dry food. I'd take the food to their eating area as Marsh leapt about over the drop spot. To keep a little control over his excitement I'd require this wiggling, wagging dog to sit and wait for my "O.K." to eat, while I took Sam her food. When Sam had hers, he could eat. But before she would eat, Sam had to have her morning massage, pats, and hugs. Then she'd study the food, sniff it a bit, give it a couple of licks, look at me, and then start her meal.

It was a similar routine with bones and treats. Marshall was always right there, jumping as high as my shoulder, whining, carried away with excitement. I'd have to give Sam her treat first, which of course, Marshall wanted to snatch away. Sam would come up and very gently receive the bone from my hand, then take it out to the grassy area. She'd set it down, still standing, study it carefully, look back at me, sniff it, lick it, look back at me, and only then settle down. Her eyes softened, her body relaxed, finally she'd begin to enjoy her treat. If Marshall got his first, he was inclined to swallow it whole so as to be ready for the opportunity to steal Sam's portion.

When we were no longer able to ride the open range with the dogs, their greatest treat became the once a week to walk with me and the trash barrel the 300 feet down the drive to the street. All I had to say was "walkies." Ears came alive. Marshall would keep talking until the gate opened and we started down the drive. To them it seemed a wilderness trek, noses exploring every bush and stone along the way. They always looked happy and fulfilled on the return; as if they'd had a mini-vacation. Since they had free run of two and a half acres, we felt they didn't need our precious time to take them on walks.

I loved Marshall, but often didn't like him too much, and wished he'd leave me alone. How could I not love someone who idolized me? He followed me everywhere, often under foot, at times tripping me and knocking me flat. He would sit and look at me in adoration. It probably began when, feeling a bit guilty for not giving him enough attention that I created "pat 'n chat time." In the evening before going up to my apartment for bed I would get Marshall to sit quietly at my feet, and speaking very softly to him, I would tell him that I loved him and that he was such a good boy as I gently stroked him for several minutes before he'd collapse over on his side. He ate it up, big time. Anticipating these sessions he would wait for me quietly each night with dreamy eyes.

Earl believed that dogs can entertain themselves with their imaginations. Sometimes he observed Marshall standing alone on the deck, looking out at a world with, seemingly, nothing going on. His tail would wag, stop for bit, then wag again for no observable reason. Earl felt certain Marshall was remembering happy days of running the hills to the stock tank, or perhaps a big bone, or going on walks, or perhaps, just enjoying the beauty of the day.

Our dogs had the best of lives. And, they brought us as much joy as we gave them.

Keebe, Arabian Princess

To my eyes there is no more glorious creature than the horse. I am thrilled to the core by an Andalusian stallion with a long flowing mane and tail displaying his grandeur, or a Lippizaner stallion from the Spanish Riding School in Vienna executing those incredible medieval maneuvers. Arabians have always been my favorite, and they are considered to be the Princes of horses. So incredible are their characteristics, that whenever any breed of horses starts to decline, a bit of Arab blood is introduced to strengthen the bloodline. Arabians can trace their ancestry back for millennia. Stories abound about their stamina, strength and gentle loving natures. So gentle are they, that often their Arab masters allowed them into their tents at night.

It is a wonder that these powerful, freedom-loving animals have made a partnership commitment to serve man. The horse opened the world for mankind. Without the horse Genghis Kahn, Alexander the Great, Marco Polo, Cortez, and others could never have expanded the civilized world. This country could never have grown in the short time it took without the horse. It was the cowboy and his horse who really opened the West.

It is a conscious partnership for horses. They thrive on our approval and praise. Whatever their job, in shows and trials, battle or working cattle, horses strive to be the best for their masters, taking pride in their accomplishments.

When I was a child, Sunday was the day the family, my mother, father and two younger sisters and I, went for a drive in the car. With great anticipation I watched for the point where the road disappeared over the hill, because I knew that just on the other side was the small corral where Shetland ponies waited for riders. Around and around the track I would fly on my steed, my heart soaring. Horses became my passion. I read horse stories, collected horse statues, and rode everywhere on my imaginary horse – even up the stairs to my bedroom. I yearned for a horse from the depth of my child's heart. I told myself that one day I would own a white Arabian.

I was fortunate in being able to spend several summer vacations on my uncle's ranch, where I was given a horse to ride and care for. In my first year at UCLA, my mother married my stepfather and moved to his ranch in Northern California. Knowing nothing about horses, they bought Gypsy for me, an unbroken horse with a streak of insanity. Even after many months of gentle handling, I was never able to touch her anywhere behind the shoulder. One day my stepfather tried to put on her halter, and she repeatedly struck at him with her front hooves, squealing loudly the entire time. Eventually, she was sent for training. It was not too effective, as shortly after her return she threw me several times, giving me a concussion. Next they bought a giant, stupid, green broke colt who didn't understand that he was to do what I wanted. Riding him was not fun. I gave up.

Since both Earl and I loved horses, one of the great attractions of moving to Wildflower Hill was that we each would buy a horse. After living all my life in large cities the thought that finally I could have my own horse thrilled me.

Earl bought a Tennessee Walker horse, Cindy, short for Syndicate, a bay horse with a rocking chair trot, from a neighbor who also had a beautiful, young, gray Arabian filly, Mirzah. It was a thrill for me to sit high up on this gorgeous, dancing, spirited creature – a challenge in control and athletic skill for me. On the day I decided to buy Mirzah it had been raining earlier and the ground was still wet. I had ridden her many times before and felt I could handle her, but my Australian stockman's saddle, which is like an English saddle, had no horn and floppy stirrups, offering little to hang onto. We were returning from a ride and Mirzah bolted, slipped and started bucking wildly, throwing me on the pavement.

I awoke on a gurney in the hospital. I hurt unbelievably, and was unable to move without great pain for over a week. That was it. I canceled my plan for ever owning a horse.

But fate had ordained that my dream would come to pass. One day in the veterinarian's waiting room with Sam, I spent the time reading messages on the bulletin board. There was a small card that read, "White Arabian mare, 13.2 hands, 19 years old, to a good home, only $500." Here was a small, older horse, cheap. Maybe I should just look at her.

Alone in the corral stood a small, white mare with a wonderful face. Kobielka, called Keebe, had always been a member of the family, a gentle lady, but with spirit. Keebe's companion horse had died, and her owner was very concerned that she find her a good home. I knew I had a wonderful home for her with a horse companion. We saddled Keebe up and after a quick trot around the yard I decided to buy her. She was smaller and closer to the ground than Mirzah. Not that far to fall, if I did.

Keebe had the traditional dish face of an Arab with large dark eyes. The surrounding black skin made it look as though she were wearing eyeliner. Being 1/8 Quarter Horse gave her a slightly larger rump than Arabs usually have, but on her it was cute. Arabians are known for their intelligence and good disposition. She had wisdom and maturity, enjoyed people, but didn't like to be hugged. Nothing happened around the place that she was unaware of. Whenever she saw me she greeted me in a low nicker that sounded like she had a sore throat. Keebe never refused anything I asked of her. Oh, she might grump, ears back and frown, but she'd do what I wanted. She never kicked, bucked, or bit – just grumped, a little. Children loved her, and she gave more gentle rides than I can count.

We already had Earl's horse, Cindy, when Keebe joined us. Cindy was the boss and Keebe was the new kid, taking second position. Cindy was much larger, and Keebe with her short legs taught herself the jog trot to keep up when we were out on a ride. Across the road from our property was BLM land leased to a cattleman and his cattle, available to us to ride. What fun we had in those days roaming the golden grassy hills over to a stock tank, with the dogs leading the way. We always took the same route, and Keebe knew the best slopes for galloping. I never had to urge her.

As our area grew, new homes were built all around us. The dirt lane in front of Wildflower Hill was paved and a new fence, without a gate, was put up. No longer were we able to ride those rolling hills. I know Keebe missed those times. Whenever we'd head out of our yard she would gaze at the far hills, her ears pricked forward. If she had her head, she'd start her jog trot in that direction.

Summertime was bounty time. Horses and chickens enjoyed lush green grass and the abundance of fruit from our numerous trees. Unfortunately, the horses often decided not to wait for the fruit to drop, but instead to pick it directly from the trees. This was forbidden fruit. In a short time Keebe became well versed in the rules, which she sometimes would break when she thought I couldn't see her, helping herself to a little fruit still on the tree. I'd yell. She'd jerk to attention, recognizing she'd been caught, put her ears back in her grump and move off – after grabbing one last quick bite. When the trees were young I painted the trunks white to protect them from sunburn. One day I noticed a peach tree with three trunks. Keebe was standing behind where she didn't think I would see her, eating peaches, until I yelled at her.

Since we had 23 fruit trees, we usually had plenty to share, except in years that had a late freeze. Horses and chickens were always willing to eat what dropped on the ground that would otherwise go to waste. The horses were experts at picking the flesh off peaches, apricots, plums and nectarines and spitting out the pits. Apples they ate seeds and all.

Horses like to pull hay from their feeders and throw it on the ground, as grazing head down is their natural posture for eating. Since our soil is sandy, eating from the ground they also pick up sand, which collects in the stomach and can cause sand colic. They will try to relieve the gas pressure and discomfort by rolling on the ground, which can twist the intestinal tract and result in death.

Cindy had a predisposition to colic. The only thing to do was to try to work through it by walking her round and round. Sometimes I've had to do this for an hour. It must have looked pretty funny to an outsider. I usually wore a big hat, man's shirt, shorts, unlaced sneakers, and carried a Circle K Thirstbuster full of ice tea. I would lead, Cindy, head hanging, shuffling behind, kicking sand into my shoes as she dragged her reluctant feet, Keebe behind her, lending support. The three of us walking 'round and 'round the corral until we were exhausted.

In fact, sand colic eventually killed Cindy. The next day a backhoe arrived and dug her very large grave, eight feet by ten feet and six feet deep, right there in the corral before pushing in the body and covering it up. Keebe had watched it all and was devastated. She grieved for Cindy, calling and calling for her.

Fortunately, within several days, Marilyn, our neighbor to the south, bought Misty. Just like Keebe, Misty was a small, white mare. From a distance you couldn't tell one from the other. Close up the difference was obvious. Misty had larger ears and smaller hooves betraying some ass in her bloodline, and sloe eyes which gave her a devious expression – as though she were planning mischief, which she often was.

Since Keebe was still grieving over the loss of Cindy, Marilyn decided to let Misty live at our place to keep Keebe company. Misty immediately took charge. Again, Keebe became number two in her own home. Misty took over the shelter. A couple of times she showed Keebe her heels, but Keebe was just happy to have a companion and accepted Misty's dominance.

Horses are not loners. In the wild a lone horse is vulnerable to predators, and this knowledge is instinctive in them; a source of fear. A horse is never happy unless there are other horses near. It used to be believed that the stallion was the head of the herd. Monty Roberts, the man who talks to horses, was probably the first to write about the hierarchy of horses, and document that it is the alpha mare who guides the herd. She is the one who teaches the young males how to behave, controlling them by eye, or by her heels if they don't get the message. The stallion's role is to protect the herd and create babies, while the alpha mare manages the herd and makes all the decisions.

After a time Marilyn moved Misty back to her place. Keebe could still see Misty and called to her constantly. Shortly after, Marilyn gave Misty to a boy who had been dreaming of having a horse, and Keebe started crying again.

Late one afternoon, coming through our front gate I heard an unfamiliar sound of "maaaa." Looking across the field to Marilyn's I saw a goat. Marilyn's new boyfriend liked goat's milk so she bought Heidi.

A couple of days later when I heard the "maaaa" continuing for hours, I picked a bit of fresh green clover and went over to introduce myself. As no one was responding to her, Heidi was feeling abandoned, no friends, no one hearing her pleading calls. Immediately, she joined me at the fence, took a couple of bites of the luscious clover, stopping when I started to pet her. I realized that she was hungry for love and affection, not food.

As I stroked her she closed her eyes and leaned against my body, ignoring my present. I ran my hands over her velvety, fawn shaded coat, admiring her ivory colored spots. Then I saw that one of her lovely, long, slim ears had ugly notch cut out of it. Undoubtedly, her original owner had slashed it as his mark of possession. It is a common practice of breeders to mutilate their animals in some particular pattern, as a cattleman might brand his cattle. I felt a great sadness for all the precious animals in the world who have suffered in this way.

A few days later as I was returning home I noticed Heidi running toward the gate. I was very flattered she would rush to meet me, until I noticed she was not interested in me but in Shadow, Marilyn's small black and white dog who had also come to the gate. When Shadow ran off Heidi followed in pursuit. The two became inseparable, never more than ten feet apart. I would see them running across the yard together, lying in the grass warming themselves in the winter sun. Happily, Heidi was no longer alone.

El Gar Rivage

Keebe desperately wanted a companion and I needed to find her one. I discovered a bulletin board in our local feed store and put up a card advertising for a roommate for Keebe. That's when Nina Ward, a stewardess, responded and brought Poco to stay with us. It seemed that the place where she had been boarding Poco had decided to keep the money she gave them by shoeing him themselves, instead of calling a farrier as she had ordered. They trimmed Poco's hooves so short that his coffin bones rotated, resulting in a condition called founder, where the tip of the bone inside the hoof presses on the soft inner sole making standing or walking extremely painful. In his misery, he stopped eating and had lost hundreds of pounds. Founder is very serious, and the vet wasn't certain Poco would ever recover. As a stewardess, Nina was gone for days at a time, so it was essential she find a new place for Poco with someone who would care about him.

Even though I had known Poco was ill, I was not prepared for the pathetic bay horse I saw when he arrived at Wildflower Hill. It was hard to believe, but I was told that he had been a show horse years before in Canada. This ugly, ewe-necked bag of bones covered with skin and hair could hardly stand, let alone put one hoof in front of another as Nina, his owner, slowly led him to the corral at his new home with us. My heart went out to this pitiful creature so obviously in pain. I resolved to do everything I could to restore him to health.

At first Keebe was rather suspicious of her new companion. Being in pain, Poco had very little interest in anything but holding on. Keebe had been living with females for many years and was extremely curious about Poco's male part. She would drop her head and stare for several minutes at a time, trying to figure out what that thing was hanging under his belly.

Keebe immediately took on the role of alpha mare. Probably for the first time in her life she was in control. Misty, her former roommate, that tough little mare, had taught her well. Keebe had learned all the tricks, and Poco was too weak to resist. She would trap him in the shelter for the night, standing so she blocked the opening. With ears back and waving her nose at him she drove him wherever she wanted. He didn't seem to be putting on weight, but I noticed she was. Then, I discovered that she was gobbling down her feed before driving him from his, so she could finish his off. At that point I realized I needed to separate them, so Earl and I built Keebe a new shelter, fencing her off from Poco.

Shortly after he arrived Poco developed a cyst on the bottom of one hoof. That meant soaking the foot in a bucket of warm Epsom salt for 20 minutes twice a day. By feeding him during the soaking time, I managed to get Poco to stand in the bucket without kicking it over. Finally, after I cured a second cyst, we got all that behind us.

Next I noticed that his spine seemed out of line and that one hip looked different than the other. I called an animal chiropractor, Dr. Maryann Gower. Poco was indeed out of alignment. I wondered how a woman would have the strength to manipulate a large horse. Standing on a stool, she grabbed Poco by the top of his neck and wagged him back and forth, pulled his tail out and pressed pressure points, quickly demonstrating her competence. Afterward she placed pulsing electrodes at crucial places. Through it all, Poco stood patiently, instinctively understanding that we were going to help him. It worked, and he was much better after the experience.

I believe the best medicine for getting any person or animal well is happiness. If I could make Poco's life a joyful one, I knew he would get well. Nina came out as often as she could to pamper him with grooming and "coffee talk," as she called it. He loved her hugs and attention. Animals respond to stroking and touching as much as do humans.

Poco became very attached to Keebe and panicked when she was out of his sight. Several times a week the two of them were allowed to roam the yard outside their corral to nibble grass and weeds and stretch their bodies. Having a best friend, few demands, a big comfortable home, special treats of carrots and fresh fruit in season made Poco a happy horse. His old spunk came back and sometimes he was even a bit brazen, banging the door impatiently when he knew food was on the way.

Slowly he got better, but it wasn't until I doubled the quantity of feed that his weight came back fully. The horse I had thought so ugly began to bloom. The crest returned to his neck, he started to remember how elegant he had been during his show career, and held his head higher.

About that time the vet said he thought Poco might be getting arthritis. Knowing that a product named MSM had become one of the new remedies for arthritis in humans I thought I'd try sprinkling it on Poco's food. About two weeks after starting the MSM, I let the horses out to trim the grass in the yard. Usually they would stroll casually from the corral. This time, as I opened the gate Poco charged out bucking and kicking and galloping around, tail in the air like a flag, head held high, stopping occasionally to snort before charging off again. He was ecstatic at having a body that, once again, felt good, and the freedom to express it.

I knew then that Poco had fully recovered, which was quite remarkable for a 26 year-old horse. When a new farrier, an old time cowboy, said he could not tell that Poco had ever had founder, and that he had never seen a horse make such a recovery, I felt elated. Poco was once again the proud, elegant, Arabian horse he once was in his show days when he was El Gar Rivage.

When he got better Nina started exercising Poco on a longe line. Keebe would watch as Poco trotted 'round and 'round Nina on the end of the line. Several years before I had tried to longe Keebe, but she didn't know what to do. She just stood at the end of the line as I waggled a long whip at her. Forgetting she didn't know how to longe, one day I hooked Keebe up to the line. She turned, walked to the end and immediately started the proper trot in a circle, as though she had done it a hundred times before. By observation, she had taught herself how to longe.

During Poco's illness Nina had called the vet. The vet, his assistant, Nina, Poco and I were standing in a circle discussing Poco's condition. Whenever there was a group in the horse yard, Keebe always joined us, watching, listening, and participating. Usually, she was acknowledged with pats, compliments and treats when people were around. In this instance, everyone was ignoring her, as Poco was the subject. Then I realized that Keebe was no longer with us. I looked around and saw her at the far corner of the yard with her fanny turned to us. She had been ignored and her feelings were hurt. I quickly remedied the situation with special attention.

We all know that it is important to stretch first thing in the morning and often rush into the day forgetting this exercise. Not Keebe. Feeding the horses is the first thing I did in the day. On the way down to the barn, Keebe'd see me and start her routine. Her front feet would go out, she'd stretch her neck and head as far as she could reach and attempt to touch her chest to the ground – the way dogs and cats stretch.

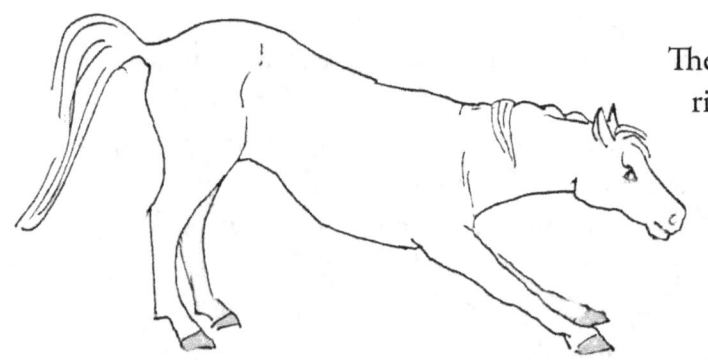

Then she'd twist her head, way to the right, then way to the left. Next, off to the end of her yard for a pee, then trotting back to her feeder, talking all the way to make certain I understood she was ready for breakfast.

In the summer, horses needed to wear screens to keep the flies off their faces. I called them "hats," a simple word the horses understood. They learned that before they got breakfast I needed to put on their hats. Poco would stretch out his neck, ears forward, but Keebe always kept her chin down and ears back. Then one morning Poco decided he wanted his breakfast first and refused his hat. I let him know it was hat first, and stood there several minutes waiting until he got the message. Hat before food was the rule. Never again did he refuse his hat.

As children, one of the first things we're told about horses is that they sleep standing up, so when you see a horse lying on the ground, legs straight out, your first thought is that the horse has died; not usually the case. There will be another horse standing close by, watching for a predator. Horses rest more completely when lying down, but in the wild there is always the danger of an attack from a predator. That instinctive memory keeps them from lying down when they are alone. Sometimes you will see a horse semi-reclining, head up, legs tucked under – more restful than standing, but down flat in a warm, sunny spot is the best rest.

Poco and Keebe became devoted to each other. She had learned much from Misty about how to be alpha mare, and she controlled Poco. Keebe played the role of mother, friend and protector. Seldom was she out of his sight for more than a few minutes, as Poco would become very distressed.

Growing up in Southern California, I never saw snow and never really experienced cold weather. Even though our area in Northern Arizona is considered to have one of the best four season climates in the country, winter always felt very cold to me. Every night it froze. I'd judge how cold it had been by how thick the ice was on the horse troughs in the morning. Sometimes it was over one inch thick, so I kept a section of 2x4 handy to whack the ice out so the horses could reach the water.

I noticed that just before sunrise Keebe would stand in the exact spot the sun's rays hit first, so she could catch its warmth as soon as it reached there. To protect themselves from the cold, horses grow heavy winter coats. As soon as the weather starts to warm, they begin to shed. My currycomb would fill after about two passes, and the hair flew about, filling the air. But, should the weather again turn cold, the shedding immediately stopped and it took a full body currying to fill the comb.

The sight of a plastic bag created great excitement for the horses. It was my practice to carry down to the barn scraps of vegetables, dried up tortillas, old muffins and the like in plastic shopping bags. The horses would eagerly shove their noses into the bag to reach the treats. The chickens, too, learned that plastic bags could mean goodies for them.

If they live long enough, horses suffer problems of aging; primarily wearing down of their teeth unevenly, which necessitates having them filed even. I noticed Poco had been holding his head in a peculiar way when he ate. Nina called her vet to have his teeth "floated," as it's called. The vet put a metal contraption into Poco's mouth to spread his jaws and keep them apart, so he could insert the file and work without losing an arm. Keebe was standing by to keep Poco calm during the process. Of course, she observed everything. At 27 years, Poco also had several loose teeth. These were not pulled, but allowed to remain and drop out in their own time. On checking, it was discovered that Keebe's teeth were even worse.

A week later the vet came back to take care of Keebe. Her teeth were badly worn, leaving hooks on the side. This time a power drill had to be used so Keebe was given a sedative. The poor girl had a hard time standing on her feet. Under sedation, her head drooped and had to be tied up to a beam so the vet could work.

It was a lengthy process. After almost an hour the sedative started to wear off. She tried to whinny through the mouth brace and then started to moan. I felt so terrible for her, but it had to be done. In the wild the condition can become so severe, with no vet to attend them that wild mustangs are no longer able to chew their food and can starve to death.

That evening, thinking that Keebe might feel comforted by spending the night with Poco in his corral, I left them together. Later I went down to check and found her standing by her gate. With a sad voice she let me know she wanted to go home to her own stall. When I opened the gate, she immediately went to her shelter.

Keebe had the help of a painkiller to weather this trauma, but for a couple of times after, when I put food in her feeder, she just rested her lips on the food unable to chew.

For several days I would see her running her tongue over her teeth, like a person exploring a new set of dentures. Within a week though, she was her old self, impatiently awaiting each morsel I brought her. To save her teeth from further wear I started feeding her small, soft senior feed and larger alfalfa pellets, which I soaked half the day in water to soften.

A new neighbor, Catherine, moved to the property that adjoined ours on the west, bringing with her two beautiful, young Arabian geldings, Trabul, a bay in brown with long white stockings and black mane and tail, and Fizah, a dappled gray. These were delightful boys who loved playing together, rearing on hind legs and pretending boy battles, then chasing each other around their corral. They were inseparable and would stand very close to each other most of the time. Being Arabs, they had a great interest in everything that went on. Whenever I walked by their yard, they'd come over to greet me and see what I was about.

One summer night about one in the morning I was awakened by a pounding sound. Getting out of bed I looked out the window to see Trabul and Fizah racing 'round and 'round their yard. I couldn't see any predators and came to the conclusion they were having fun chasing each other in the cool evening – just joyful exuberance in the moonlight.

As we did, Catherine would let her horses out of their corral to graze her property. One day I had let Keebe and Poco out to nibble the yard as I worked in the garden. All of a sudden I heard Keebe squealing loudly. Fearing she might be hurt I ran toward her. Neck arched, she was striking at the air with her front hooves as she continued the squeals. The Arabs from next door were at the fence wanting to be friendly and get acquainted, wondering what all the commotion was about. I knew. Keebe, who considered herself alpha mare, was trying to protect her herd, Poco and herself, from these strange horses. She took her job as leader very seriously. The boys were not part of her herd and were not to come too close. Catherine called her horses in, and Poco and Keebe returned to peaceful grazing. Keebe had the same reaction to another neighbor, a miniature black horse who wore a pretty red halter. Keebe would look at him, stamp her foot and squeal.

One day Catherine sold Fizah, leaving Trabul alone. He would call to Keebe and Poco, anxious to join them. Maybe because he was alone, Keebe now felt him to be acceptable to join her herd. I would see her walk to the fence and gaze across at him for several minutes at a time. I think she was saying that he had passed his probationary period and she would now accept him into her herd. That never happened, even though the lonely Trabul wanted it. He continued to call to Keebe, but Catherine put up a new fence to keep them further apart.

Trabul was an incredibly beautiful horse, always impeccably groomed, who loved to race around his corral. Watching him was seeing perfection in motion. You could feel the joy in his heart, as he galloped, feet flying, with head and tail held high. Then his shelter came down, and the next day he was gone. I really missed him. Catherine did not get along with her neighbors, so I never knew what happened to him. Later she moved away, and that saga ended.

Garden Spirits

Almost as important to us as the animals, were the gardens. We had moved to Wildflower Hill because we wanted to grow our own food and live in off the land. And, we wanted to do this in harmony with nature, growing organically and naturally, mimicking nature as much as we were able.

Since we were city folk, we had a lot to learn. I bought books on organic gardening and natural ways to fertilize and counter pest attacks. In the beginning, Wildflower Hill had one established vegetable garden with a mature asparagus patch. My goal was to grow every kind vegetable possible, raise medicinal herbs, and all the varieties of fruit trees that grew in our area.

We were fortunate to have a good well that was 400 feet deep, which meant that it took about seven years for water to percolate down from the surface, assuring the filtering out of most toxins. However, in a crisis we needed a reliable power source to pump the water to the surface, so we bought a generator. Since we had chickens, they and their eggs could be a continuing source of protein in an emergency. With over a hundred trees on the property we had a pretty reliable source of fuel, should we need it to cook and for heat. We figured we had covered all our bases.

Since the first thing we had done was to plant more fruit trees we now had a total of 25. Next I wanted additional gardening space. That first fall I selected two areas for new gardens and covered the virgin prairie with sawdust, chicken manure, horse manure and alfalfa hay, then added fishing worms I bought at a Circle K, dug it all in and watered it thoroughly. In the spring we were rewarded with beautiful rich, pliable soil that included many more precious earthworms. Earl enclosed the spaces with fencing and we were set. I now had a total of three garden spaces with room for exotic herbs like licorice root, ashwaganda, echinacea, and other flights of fancy, as well as sunflowers and roses to dress things up. I made the gateways too narrow for the horses, who would have loved to feast on all the delectables.

Now ready for business, I called on the nature spirits and devas to assist me in maintaining healthy and abundant gardens. In the Native American tradition, I recognized that without the help of these spirits there would be no gardens, and if I acknowledged them and called for their help, everything would prosper. Each plant has a deva to guide its development, and nature spirits to do the work of assisting the growth.

Because all of life is precious to me, and I believe everything has a consciousness, it was my practice to speak to my flowers, herbs and vegetables, plants and trees. I blessed them and told them they were greatly valued, and that I desired them to be healthy and happy. They, too, were my kids at Wildflower Hill.

Then each fall on the solstice I held a thanksgiving ceremony, as I had been taught by my Cherokee friend, Cheryl. I brought into the orchard some dried corn and beer, and burned sage to purify the area. At this point I would call the nature spirits, devas and Pan, the god of fields and plants, to my party. I gave thanks and appreciation to them for the year's bounty. In my mind, I could see them dancing and hear them giggling with glee.

As part of my preparation for the next year I put my gardens to bed each year under a blanket of horse and chicken manure, together with some alfalfa. In the spring, when the frost was gone and my spade turned the earth, I had to spend a lot of time covering up the multitude of earthworms teeming in my soil, so the sun wouldn't kill them. I always blessed them for the good work they did fertilizing my soil with their precious poop.

The gardens blessed everyone. The horses and chickens loved the fruit. Cooked vegetables I added to the dogs' food. Grubs, bugs and grasshoppers I collected by hand for the chickens, and boy, did they love them. All I had to do was walk toward the chicken yard with my hand held out, and every hen would run – full tilt – toward the fence for a tasty handout.

I never had a garbage problem. If the animals didn't eat it, I buried it in the garden to enrich the soil – just another way to compost and return to the earth.

You could think of Wildflower Hill as a cooperative. Nature and I planted the seeds, the horses and chickens provided the manure, earthworms cultivated and added their fertilizer, and the bees would pollinate. The birds, lizards and toads kept down the pests, and the horses mowed the grass to keep down the weeds.

To most people used to orderly rows in a garden, mine probably looked like an undisciplined disaster. Flowers and herbs and vegetables mixed naturally, as they might in the wild. Plants were allowed to go to seed, and their babies dispersed themselves in carpets and meandered into corners or under other plants. Letting plants go to seed simplified planting, and all I needed to do was thin or transplant them to give the strong ones space to develop. I always took into consideration that certain plants enhance the health of others. Calendula and marigolds kept bugs off beans and other plants, but carrots hate dill, so they needed to be kept apart. I hoped random planting might confuse pests who were used to marching down a row, instead of having to search for the next plant. About the only order you'd see was in the perennial rows of artichokes, asparagus, and in the beans I planted along the fence. Since I could never find all the potatoes, they might reappear the next spring anywhere, between the onions or bursting up in the middle of the carrots.

I knew the nutritional value of dandelion greens, and that their roots had medicinal powers. There were no dandelions at Wildflower Hill, so one day when I was in town I found someone's yard full of dandelions, picked the seed heads to spread about my garden. Since they were wanted, the dandelions grew very lush and beautiful with large roots that I dried for herbal tonics.

My gardens were a paradise for plants and creatures of all sorts, as well as humans. Nature had created our area as prairie grassland; not originally designed for vegetables, flowers, herbs and orchards. However, Wildflower Hill became an oasis for birds looking for water and food to survive our hot, dusty summers and freezing winters. They in turn helped keep the pests under control. I was careful not to use poisons on my plants so they could safely raise healthy babies – which we had in abundance.

I believe all of Nature shared the blessings of Wildflower Hill.

Precious Poop

Without intestinal bacteria and soil based organisms, we could not digest our food and would die. Among other benefits, a good supply of the bacteria can delay the aging process. I have seen foals eating their mother's manure, which apparently, they need to build the right digestive bacteria into their own bodies.

All our chicken and horse manure went into the gardens to feed my plants. Samantha and Marshall would watch as I filled up the wheelbarrow in the corral, and they were right there when I stopped in the garden. They'd poke their noses in and pick out what they considered to be choice pieces. Very selective of the manure, not the freshest or the driest material, they'd carefully test each piece by sniff and touch until they found properly aged pieces. Like choosing a fine cheese, I guess.

Sam at 11 years and Marshall at 10 appeared to be about half their ages. Their real ages in human years were about 70 and 66. Yet, they would romp and play with the energy of young dogs. Tawny, the dog next door, Sam's age, had been gray for several years and acted like an old lady.

Since the neighbors did not have horses it occurred to me that perhaps Tawny was missing some essential intestinal flora that our dogs got. I started tossing a little manure over the fence to her. Whenever she saw me coming with a shovel of manure, she excitedly danced in circles. You would have thought I had brought her fillet mignon the way she gobbled it up. I think she probably needed it.

One year I kept our new chicks in their special yard much longer than previously, until they were fully mature. When I opened the gate so they could join the flock, the first thing they did was to head for the fresh horse manure and gobble great bites.

Almost nothing went to waste at Wildflower Hill. The old timers knew how to live in harmony with the land. As the consummate expert on recycling, Mother Nature has planned everything magnificently. An excellent fertilizer is composted organic material. So, of course, I composted as much as I could. However, as we lived in a very dry climate I had difficulty keeping the compost pile the right degree of moisture. Since I wanted to do everything the easy way, I composted directly in the ground. With the exception of the heaviest, largest pruning and cuttings, which I burned, returning the ash to the soil, I buried my green vegetable waste material. I'd dig a hole, drop in scraps of vegetables and old bread, toss in a bit of manure and cover it up. With no effort on my part, nature and the earthworms went to work, and within a couple of weeks the garbage was gone, replaced by light soil reeling with a tangle of beautiful earthworms who were making the finest fertilizer there is.

I highly valued the hard-working worms. In the spring and fall, particularly, my soil teemed with these little guys. When the weather was mild, neither baking hot or freezing cold, they came closer to the surface. Digging could turn up hundreds of them in a shovel full. Since exposure to the sun would kill them, I spent considerable time covering up the ones that landed on top of the dirt.

Chicken manure is very rich in nutrients. Our first year at Wildflower Hill, I killed most of my strawberry plants because I didn't realize its power and liberally spread it over the strawberries, ignorantly thinking more was better. Within a short time the tender plants shriveled back and died. Believe me, after that I gave poop more respect. If you want to use the fresh stuff, make poop tea. A gallon of water in a plastic milk container, with a couple of tablespoons of chicken manure, aged a week, can be used directly on plants. My tomatoes had never seemed to reach the size I thought they could, until I buried chicken manure in a trench I had dug along side the plants. When the roots reached the manure the tomato plants practically leaped forward, doubling their size.

As a child I remembered reading in Life magazine of a rancher who had injured his leg. Being a savvy old guy, he knew about primitive penicillin. He stuffed his boot with cow manure and shoved his leg inside. Within a short time the leg healed completely.

You don't need to put manure in your boot or eat poop. Your health food store has more acceptable forms of beneficial intestinal bacteria which everyone needs. Doctors have abused antibiotics to the point that we are reaching a crisis. Perhaps we should return to nature for safe remedies that have no side effects. Each month I hear new horror stories about how chemical companies try to make gardeners more dependent upon their poisonous sprays and chemical fertilizers. All these products have devastating long term effects on soil and its precious microorganisms. As for me,

I'll stick to gardening the old fashioned way with Mother Nature's microorganisms, earthworms and precious poop.

My Quandary

To kill or not to kill, that was my quandary. Whether 'tis better to suffer being overwhelmed by mice, ground squirrels, moles, rabbits, ants, grasshoppers, blister beetles and others, or to "off" them, that was the question which plagued me. I have a great reverence for all life and recognize that everything was created for a purpose... even though I may not know why we must endure mosquitoes and the like. For many years I tolerated ant nests, but when the number rose to 10 large colonies, and after big, black ants bit me repeated times I decided it was war. The pain from just one bite could be quite acute for many hours. I spoke to the colonies and told them I honored their right to life, but I wished them to move off my land, and if after two weeks they hadn't moved I would take drastic steps.

When, after two weeks they were still there, I attacked the most prominent nest. For a start I began flooding it with water. Then it was a heavy dose of diatomaceous earth, which they don't like. They remained. Chopping the soil to cave in their subterranean rooms didn't work either. I would not use poisons to kill them, as I was very protective of my soil. I finally gave up, and they seemed to back off, too.

 Puddie Pie, our first cat, was a good mouser. After he disappeared, I tried to introduce Menehuni Mittens to the challenge of hunting mice. When I discovered a mouse in a feed bin, I showed it to her. She was terrified and struggled hard to get away in a hurry. Unfortunately, birds were her sport.

I was reduced to setting mousetraps. Peanut butter was the best bait in a snap trap. Fortunately, I believe most of the mice died quickly as the bar usually caught them across the neck. It was always sad for me to find one of these miniature mammals with its life snuffed out, tiny toes curled up, ears laid back with eyes closed, but I couldn't let them take over the place, which they could easily do given the number of children and grandchildren and great grandchildren they produce in one year. Before disposing of a body, I always blessed it and released its soul to heaven, hoping it didn't leave a family behind.

Help with the mouse situation appeared from an unexpected quarter. Imagine my surprise as I entered the feed room of the barn almost stepping on a snake, a beautiful red racer. It was as shocked to see me as I was to see it. Immediately, it found a corner where it wound its long, slim body into a tangle of loops. Many of the traps I had set, I was finding across the room and empty. Possibly, the snake was cleaning out the traps, and removing the mice for me.

Rabbits aren't usually a problem when you have dogs. A rabbit may venture in, nibble a few bites on a vegetable until it sees a dog, then it's a mad dash by both until the rabbit dives through the fence to safety.

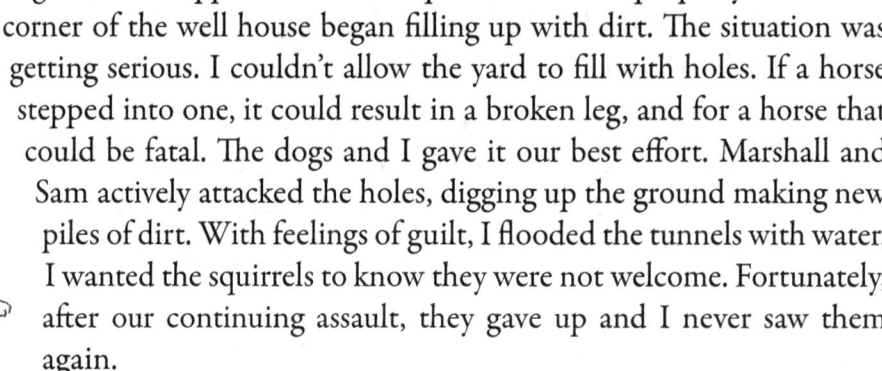

One day, I noticed the area under the horse trough filling up with loose dirt and a hole appeared in the middle of the corral. I didn't know who the culprit was – until one morning out of the corner of my eye – I saw a furry grey flash disappear under the water trough. Was it a ground squirrel? Later that day I noticed one of the concrete blocks I had stacked to form a wall had been knocked down and Marshall was very disturbed by something. As I approached the scene, a very angry ground squirrel popped out of a block and barked furiously at us before scampering off. Holes appeared in several places about the property, and even a corner of the well house began filling up with dirt. The situation was getting serious. I couldn't allow the yard to fill with holes. If a horse stepped into one, it could result in a broken leg, and for a horse that could be fatal. The dogs and I gave it our best effort. Marshall and Sam actively attacked the holes, digging up the ground making new piles of dirt. With feelings of guilt, I flooded the tunnels with water. I wanted the squirrels to know they were not welcome. Fortunately, after our continuing assault, they gave up and I never saw them again.

I do revere life unless it's June bugs, which one year stripped most of the leaves from a fruit tree, or blister beetles, which regularly decimated my potato plants, or the grasshoppers who eat anything. Without poison, it's hard to handle these invasions. I made a spray from garlic, onions, cayenne pepper, and dish soap, which can be effective to a degree, not killing but driving them away, usually to the neighbors. In the cool of

 the morning I could find grasshoppers sitting on the sunflowers or bean vines, waiting for the sun to warm their bodies so they could move. This was a great time to easily grab them by hand, and save them in a coffee can. With great glee, I delighted the chickens with this fresh meat. Anticipating these special treats, the chickens would rush to the fence to meet me, ready for the feast. These big fat hoppers I'd feed from my hand one by one to the hens, who'd grab and run off to keep their prize from the other girls.

One year I had the challenge of moles in my vineyard. By continually flooding their tunnels with water I convinced them they were not welcome and they retreated. Each year at Wildflower Hill brought new and different challenges. Each year a star nemesis – drought, bugs, predators – always something new. But it was all worth it; part of the price we had to pay to enjoy the bounty of wonderful fruits, vegetables, herbs, and the joy of our animal companions.

Year of the Birds

It may have begun when I decided to buy an incredible Native American fetish necklace, which consisted of 17 beautiful wild birds made entirely from semi-precious stones. Each detail was carved in a different colored stone – beaks, tails, wings, crests – as many as six different stones on one bird. After I got home, I spent some time marveling at this marvelous creation, praising the talent of its artist, and blessing the real life birds whose beauty was being celebrated.

Cheryl "Laughing Wolf" taught me that Native Americans use the fetish to attract an animal. And, that year we had five times as many birds as we had previously seen – with varieties we'd never had before at Wildflower Hill. At one time I counted nine active nests and I knew there were many more. Everyone seemed to be making babies.

Eight years earlier Earl had built a charming four-plex birdhouse in the style of a barn. No birds had ever inhabited it, which had crushed him. However this year, a male house wren I called Buster advertised for weeks from the roof for a mate. Finally, Suzie joined him and the two successfully raised a family in Earl's birdhouse.

All spring we were serenaded with bird songs. For the first time we seemed to be spared some of the insect infestations we had grown to expect as the mothers and fathers fed their growing broods with the bugs they picked from my young vegetables and fruit trees. So, that year we had a bumper crop of fruit. Earl worried that the birds would devastate the cherry crop, but there was plenty for everyone. Besides, it was nice to feed the bird families. Robins, in particular, are very fond of cherries, as are the chickens, dogs, horses and people.

Water is vital to all life and can be hard to find in a dry prairie. Our sprinklers ran every day in the summer, a great attraction for birds who wanted a shower – and I was careful to keep the birdbath filled – yet, unfortunately, several birds drowned trying to quench their thirst at the horse trough. One day, when the level was low, I found a young bird sitting in the trough barely keeping its head above the water, too exhausted from its struggle to get out. I carefully picked him out, dried him on my shirt and tucked him under my arm. I carried him to a pine tree, gently set him upon a branch and backed away. After 10 minutes he had recouped his strength and flew off.

It's a miracle that bird populations survive, when so many babies die. Eggs often didn't hatch, babies fell out of nests, predators got them, they drowned in horse troughs, and some I found dead for whatever reason. In a year I might find eight to ten little bodies, and who knows how many others I didn't find. When they didn't survive, I felt such sadness for the parents who had invested so much of themselves to produce these little lives.

By midsummer, fledglings had grown and the chatter and flutter died down. The sparrows, which always flew around in large noisy clusters, disappeared for a while. One species that particularly delighted me were the very small peeps, not much larger than a hummingbird. Each evening they would feast on the seeds of the wild sunflowers that I let grow in the gardens. With fertile soil and plenty of water, the flowers grew to eight feet, instead of the three feet they reached in ditches along the roads.

Flowers, in addition to adding beauty perform a useful service. They are permitted among my vegetables, because they draw bees which pollinate the plants, which later produce seeds to nourish the birds.

Hummingbirds stayed as long as there was nectar. What a wonder they are! It's unbelievable that they are able to survive at all with such high energy requirements. I've heard they must find food every four hours, and only make it through the night by going into a state of hibernation. From our screened porch we could watch them at the feeder. They sound like mini-weed-eaters and reminded me of Jedi pilots with their incredible maneuvers. For a while, the feeder was fiercely defended by a lone bee, which was able to drive off these much larger flying machines, which, in turn, would drive off each other.

My favorites were the mourning doves – so very gentle and sweet. They could be seen for most of the year casually strolling about the yard; they never hop. In the spring they would build ridiculous nests – a few pine needles in the crotch of a tree branch – then, for two weeks, sit day and night on a couple of eggs. Often a wind came up and blew away the puny nest and eggs, and the dove would start all over again, build another nest, and sit for another couple of weeks. It was pathetic to see such devotion unrewarded.

Late one summer day while driving down the highway, I spied a bundle of feathers along side the road. Cheryl had said, per Native American tradition, when you see road kill with a wing pointing up, it is a sign that you are to collect the body and save the parts. The Native Americans say that the bird is honoring you and should be honored in return. At first I thought it was a hawk. When I turned the head I saw it was a barred owl. The wide open eyes sent a shock wave directly into my heart and I felt an immediate connection from these deep, dark pools. It was very beautiful and perfect with no visible injury, although it was definitely dead. In the Indian way I "released its spirit to heaven." The beautiful wings, tail and claws I preserved, and later gave them to my friend Morningstar to use in her ceremonies. I then thanked it for honoring me. That night I dreamed of the owl, who said his name was Orion and that he would be my protector.

Several months later I thought of the bird and chided myself that it was merely a romantic fantasy that a dead owl could in any way protect me. Then I heard an inner voice telling me that he was my protector on the spiritual plane, the other side. If one believes in such thing as evil spirits, curses, and negative energy, then to have a spiritual protector is a great blessing. So I spoke to Orion and told him I was grateful that he would be my protector, and I gave him my permission to look after me from the spirit world. Then I realized that since he had entered my life I had been feeling incredibly free and whole – no longer beset by nagging feelings of anxiety, fear, worry, or any of the ordinary disturbances that affect most people. Was this due to Orion's protection from negative energy?

Could my fetish necklace have brought all this wonder into my life? This "Year of the Birds" connected me strongly to the "winged-ones," as Native Americans call them. I will always appreciate the very important job they perform in saving our food from devastation by the hoards of insects and other creatures that could otherwise devastate our crops. Look closely the next time you see birds close by; give them thanks and honor. Drink in their beautiful plumage and love songs that divinely bless all our lives.

The Eggs and I

From the first day at Wildflower Hill, collecting eggs had always been a delight, an ongoing treasure hunt. Since I wrote into our purchase contract that the previous owner should leave her chickens, we had eggs from day one. Each day I'd wonder, how many will there be today? What colors will they be? Since the Aracanas lay blue or green eggs, and the others lay shades from white through cream to brown, the collection made a beautiful array of colors on the golden hay of a nest.

As we kept around 20 hens, we always had more eggs than we could use, so I sold the extras. A new customer would frequently complain that the yolks were orange. I then would proudly tell them that my hens got good feed and had a wonderful meadow where they picked fresh greens, grubs and bugs for protein. Supermarket eggs from hens kept crowded in wire cages are pale yellow. My girls had happy lives and produced, so I was told, the very best eggs in town.

Even though we had many nesting boxes, hens always seemed to want the same one. Two hens might get in together, with one, two or three waiting. Everyone knows they are waiting, because they're quite vocal about it – making loud clucking, sobbing sounds that go on and on until space becomes available. The hens issue urgent squawks that can be heard across the yard. Sometimes I would find an egg lying on the floor of the hen house and knew that one hen had not been able to wait for her turn at the nesting box, and had given birth on the floor.

The laying of an egg is an interesting process. The hen chooses her spot and customizes it. She may turn round and round to make a depression in the straw before plopping down in the center, then may pick up pieces of straw and tuck them next to her body. At this point, she gets very quiet, entering what appears to be a state of meditation, often lasting half an hour. When the egg is ready to be delivered, the hen will stand and let it drop onto the hay. As it passes through the birth canal, it is given a wet, protective coating. She will stand over it for couple of minutes as the coating dries, before announcing to the world her great accomplishment with several loud clucks as she struts off.

On occasion, a hen would decide she wanted a private place in which to lay. Dalmatia, a black and white spotted hen, was the sneakiest. Because she was small, she could fly to the rafters and over into another part of the barn, squeeze behind a bale of hay, or find some loose straw for her personal spot. It might take days or weeks before I found the place, but when the number of eggs would drop off I suspected there was a hidden nest somewhere.

Apricot got top prize for hiding eggs. After I emptied the feedbags, it was my habit to store them on a shelf above the straw bales. One day I saw Apricot exit from behind the bags. Stretching my hand up to the spot I felt an egg. Ah ha, I thought. Reaching up again, felt several more. By the time I collected them all I had 59 eggs. Since an egg a day is heavy production, Apricot must have been laying there for a couple of months. Quite a stash!

I never liked to see anything go to waste. After all, Apricot had worked very hard to produce all those eggs, and I appreciated them. By putting the eggs in water, I was able to determine which were fresh, as a fresh egg will lie on the bottom. If an egg floats, it is well past prime. Even though during World War II some of our troops were fed eggs that had been stored in a salt mine since 1939, my customers came to me for fresh eggs, so I didn't feel I could sell them old eggs; besides, I didn't have a salt mine. These older eggs I fed to the dogs, who weren't picky about the age of their eggs.

Generally, hens lay in the morning or early afternoon. When I saw a hen sitting on a nest around sunset, I'd suspect she was trying to set her eggs. In the spring we often had at least one young hen who felt an urge for motherhood. If I allowed her to set, at the end of each day she would have additional eggs from all the other hens. She would use her wing to move any egg laid beside her to under her body. I could never tell which were the new eggs and which were the nester's eggs. I would have no eggs to sell if I didn't collect them each day.

When I was particularly touched by a hen's desire for babies, I'd make special arrangements for her to set in a separate place to complete the 21-day cycle to chicks. Often the eggs wouldn't hatch. When they did, something unfortunate usually seemed to happen to the chicks. For several years our dog, Sam, would ambush the babies who often managed to squeeze through the fence. It broke my heart to find these little dead bodies. I decided the best way to raise chicks is to buy them, set them up in a nursery where I could manage them and insure their survival.

I remember the time I found Matilda on the nest each evening. For several days, I removed the eggs from under her as she strongly protested. I realized that she wanted to raise some babies. She seemed so determined that I didn't have the heart to deny her chance at motherhood. To keep her eggs from being mixed with new ones laid by other hens, I moved her to a special room. It was amazing. She sat there, day after day, in a meditative state, never seeming to leave. I didn't think she was eating or drinking, so I put food and water beside her, which slowly disappeared. After five weeks and no chicks, I knew it just wasn't going to happen. Either the eggs had not been kept warm or they had been infertile. I disposed of them and put Matilda out with the other hens. Later I saw her sitting in the yard making a strange sound, something like crying. I believe she was mourning the loss of her unborn children.

Another covert mother was more successful. While getting hay for the horses one evening, I heard little chirping voices. There, behind the stacked hay bales were three baby chicks and 14 eggs hidden in a manger. As there was no way for them to get out, without food and water they would have perished had I not found them. I set the chicks on the floor. Mom rushed in and took charge, escorting them out to join the rest of the flock.

Another time, upon entering the barn, I heard a peep, peep, peep. I couldn't imagine. It sounded like a chick. I opened the door to the nesting room and saw a newly hatched chick on the shelf four feet above the floor. No way it could have flown up from the floor, and I knew no hen had been nesting there for three weeks. It could only have come from above. Its mother must have been setting in the ceiling, and baby dropped down after hatching, fortunately falling into a soft bed of hay on the shelf. At that point, mother heard the call, came rushing in from the yard to claim her baby, who I had placed on the floor. Mom then took baby out to proudly show off to the other hens.

I didn't encourage nesting hens, but if the hen managed it in secret, I wouldn't deny her motherhood.

Polly & Wolly

One year I decided to handle the baby chicks in hope that they would come to fear me less. My star pupils were two Rhode Island reds I named Polly and Wolly Doodle. Polly became my favorite, and I was able to pick her up any time I chose. She even became quite brazen, running in my path to get attention, and often getting stepped on. Since she had no fear of humans she had no reluctance to get into everything – quite a brat at times.

Being totally fearless, she did whatever she wanted and I was constantly challenged, trying to figure ways to control her. Polly even became so confident of her rights that she started laying eggs in the horse feeders. She understood that flying into feeders was not permitted, but hey, she wanted to, so she did. I had to physically grab her and throw her out. The real challenge came when she decided that Poco's feeder was the perfect place to spend the night. I wouldn't have minded so much if she hadn't left packages of poop by morning.

In addition to alfalfa, the horses were fed special pellets of concentrated nutrition. As they chewed, small bits fell from their mouths to the ground. The chickens, always waiting below the feeders, quickly cleaned up what dropped. Polly figured out that the source of the food was the feeder high above. One day I had just put pellets into Keebe's feeder and she was nibbling away, when she whirled and charged out of her shelter. Polly, realizing Keebe had pellets, decided not to wait for them to drop and flew up into the feeder. The flapping of wings in her face had terrorized Keebe and she fled. Standing about 15 feet away, she was afraid to reclaim her dinner. I grabbed Polly and threw her out, and it took a bit of coaxing to bring Keebe back.

The problem was solved shortly after when Polly was stepped on by one of the horses and her leg broken. As I always did with broken legs, I set her up by herself with plenty of food and water. It was a severe break, and weeks before she was able to hobble about on her newly bowed leg. However, it did take some of the sass out of her and she no longer flew into horse feeders.

Polly always saw me as I approached the barn, and when I opened the door to the chicken yard, she immediately popped up to join me, demanding I personally feed her corn scratch from my hand. She would even stand on the tips of my shoes, tilting back, looking me straight in the eye. Of course, I couldn't resist and always grabbed a little extra for her, which made her even more demanding. If I didn't respond quickly, she would peck the corn in my hand extra hard. I got the idea she was punishing me for not being prompt enough.

I was cleaning out the hay room getting ready for a new load, when Polly clucked at me from her roost on the other side of the inside window, asking to join me. I let her in and she immediately started examining the entire room. She checked into all the corners, hopped on the edge of a bucket, tipping it over, pecked at the mousetrap, clucking the whole time. Then, moving into the adjoining storage room, she found where I had loose straw stored in the manger. Her voice suddenly became soft and gentle as she started to hollow out a nest in the hay. It was the voice of a mother hen to her chicks. It sounded as though she was talking to herself about the babies she was thinking about having. Finally, she settled in and all was quiet. However, as soon as the egg was laid she loudly announced its arrival to the world and left. I felt a bit let down. There would be no baby Pollys.

Polly continually demonstrated an intelligence superior to the other hens. I wondered if my conversations with her might have stimulated the growth of extra connectors in her brain. Scientists have discovered that stimulating a human child's brain can appreciably increase that child's intelligence. Could it work with chickens, too?

Lizbet, a large, golden-feathered hen was at the top of the pecking order, and she advertised this to the world with her loud squawking. It wasn't until her late years that I noticed her legs splaying out, and within a short time she found it difficult to walk, developing the posture of a vulture, hunching her shoulders and dragging her tail on the ground. In all those years was she complaining about painful hip joints?

Not wanting to miss out on any food treats I gave the other girls, she continued to drag herself around. No longer able to fly up onto a roost at evening, she spent her nights huddled in a corner of the hen house. I knew life was rather painful for her and wondered if I should put her down.

Reluctantly, I thought about it for days, finally I decided that I would dispatch her on Sunday. I sharpened my ax and found a bag for her body. Wanting to delay things,

I decided to clean the chicken house first. Always when I cleaned the chicken house all the hens would move outside, but on this day Lizbet decided to join me, sitting in the corner. I told her that I would soon send her to heaven. She listened quietly. The door to the ante room was open and she waddled in and sat on the bag beside the ax, waiting.

Finally, I could no longer put off the inevitable, the moment had arrived. Usually, when I picked up a hen they flapped hysterically and screamed their heads off. I had never been able to touch Lizbet before, but now she let me pick her up with no resistance. I held her close and told her the time had come, and thanked her for all the wonderful eggs she had given us. I blessed her, picked up the ax and bag and we moved outside. I put her in the bag, leaving her head out. Ordinarily, this would result in frantic flapping and hysterical screams from the hen, but she remained quiet. I swung my ax and it was over. Nobody can tell me she didn't know what was going on; and she had been ready.

Ducky-Doo and Friends

Each spring when I visited our local feed store to buy newborn chicks, I was particularly enchanted by the baby ducks. Finally, one year I succumbed and bought four. I had hoped for a boy and three girls. The first white Peking I knew was a boy, and named him Ducky-Doo. The second Peking, who spent more time than the other three together bathing and preening to pristine white perfection, I named Angel. When Angel turned out to be a male, his name became Angelo. Carmella looked like a caramel sundae with her mixture of white and caramel feathers. Artemeda was a mallard in lovely shades of brown.

Totally ignorant about ducks, I hadn't known they couldn't swallow their food without large quantities of water. As soon as Earl told me, I bought them a little wading pool and drinking pond all in one. Their small size posed a problem for them getting in and out of a pool. The solution came with a painter's tray. I made a little step to assist them in hopping up to the high end of the tray, and then they could walk down the ramp into the water. This wonderful solution only worked for a couple of weeks. Ducks grow twice as fast as chickens and they quickly outgrew this little pond.

Upon graduation to a child's 36" wading pool, their imaginations took off. They'd race-swim around the perimeter and do dunk-dives as though it was a large lake. Back on the ground after a swim, with necks stretched skyward, each would do an in-place flapping of wings to dry, which lifted him on web footed toes. It always reminded me of WWII fighter pilots revving up their engines before takeoff.

Water was their lifeline as well as their joy. At feeding time on cold winter mornings all four would come running up to tell me that I needed to break the ice on their pond. The minute I did, four little heads would dunk in and start "schnibbling" the water and eating the ice. Only then would they have any interest in food – water first, food second.

They spent most of the day in an adjoining meadow. Originally part of the horse corral, I fenced it off so that native grasses and wildflowers could restore the desert from what the horses had made of the land. The first spring brought forth an astonishing array of plants on ground that had been well fertilized by horses and chickens for several years. This plot became a Garden of Eden for domestic and wild birds, as well as my ducks. The two females would sit very close together continually chatting, reminding me of little girls having a tea party.

When Angel became Angelo, he also became a bully, chasing the hens, taking them down and beating them up – so he was dispatched to duck heaven. I felt badly that I didn't have a lake for Ducky-Doo, Carmella and Artemeda, as the wading pool had become too small for grown ducks. Ralph and Julie next door had an enormous stock tank. Ralph had built a long ramp up to the top so his ducks could easily reach the water. It was the perfect life for ducks. They could join together doing deep dives, swimming and playing together endlessly. So, Ducky-Doo and his girlfriends moved to Ralph's where they enjoyed many years of ducky bliss.

Earl and I went to visit Patty Woodruff, who lived in a beautiful, green oasis fed by an artesian well, virtually unheard of in the dry landscape we lived on. This was the perfect Eden for wild and domestic animals, including geese. We were chatting together with her husband, soaking up the beauty of their shaded glen, when a handsome Toulouse goose strolled by. I found him very beautiful in his elegance and exclaimed out loud how magnificent I found him to be. He listened, looked at me and started parading back and forth before me with great confidence and pride. I told him that I wished I had such a wonderful goose and continued with my admiration. He watched me, then sized Earl up, recognizing that I already had a mate in Earl. He hung around joining in the conversation occasionally, but when we started to leave he launched an attack on Earl. It was obvious that he considered Earl his competition for my affection.

Death

Death came for Lacey on a snowy, winter day. I had noticed a few days before that she seemed detached and disinterested in the world around her. She chose to stand apart from the other chickens, and didn't run for scratch with them. One evening after all the girls had hit their roosts for the night, I found Lacey, head tucked down, feathers fluffed against the cold, sitting outside on the snow as the day dimmed. I picked her up, carried her into the henhouse and set her in a cozy spot on some straw in a nesting box.

In the morning I found her on the floor sitting in front of the open small chicken house doorway where the snow had blown in. She was resting quietly. I then understood she was waiting for death. I wondered if she had planned to go quicker by sitting in the snow the night before, and remembered stories about indigenous tribes where the elders, deciding their time had come, would go out into the wilderness to wait for death. Perhaps that was what Lacey had intended. Maybe I had interfered with her plan and delayed her going. When I went down to feed in the late afternoon I found she had left her body, which was still lying in the same spot where she had spent the night.

Lacey taught me how to recognize when a chicken is getting ready to die. They have no interest in food, but slow down, mostly sit and wait. In the beginning I used to worry that it was an illness, which it never was. From time to time I would find an alert hen staying in one spot for a while. That often turned out to be a broken leg – usually a horse had stepped on her. If possible, I'd try to make the infirmed hen comfortable in a nest with bowls of water and feed close by, until, within a couple of days, the hen would be hobbling about again.

It's always difficult when a precious creature dies, but death comes to every living thing eventually, and when an animal has lived its full lifespan, it's easier to accept. But when I find a baby bird that has fallen from a nest or drowned in the horse trough, it tears my heart.

It was tough on Earl when his horse Cindy succumbed to sand colic. She had been a gentle and willing partner on many a happy ride across the grassy hills. A Tennessee

Walker horse with a smooth gait, like riding in a rocking chair, she would never be replaced. When she was buried in the corral, Earl expressed his appreciation and gave thanks to her with his goodbye. Keebe, her companion, watched and I knew her heart was heavy, too, as she cried for days afterwards.

Iswan was a handsome, seal brown Arabian Stallion, who was almost Champion of Champions. On the day of the competition for Top Ten in the prestigious Scottsdale Arabian Show, someone, who obviously considered him an important contender and threat, drugged him. Because he was unable to compete, he had to be withdrawn and was unable to claim the glory that might have been his. But he was the grand champion to his beloved friend and owner, Patty Woodruff. More than a horse, he was a friend who always knew what she wanted. Acting with dignity, he was consistently a gentleman with the mares that were brought to him.

At the age of 33, arthritis in one hoof and a hip brought closure to his breeding days. In appreciation Patty allowed him the run of her place, the joy of companionship with her mares, and his feeder always full of hay.

By age 35 it was apparent that Iswan's life was coming to an end. His elimination systems were shutting down. He was in pain. Patty knew it was time to end his suffering and called the vet. After considerable thought she decided on a spot in a far pasture for his gravesite.

When the vet arrived they found that, on his own, Iswan had picked his way through several gateways, over a difficult crossing and was waiting for them, standing on the very spot Patty had chosen for his grave. I will always wonder, did he know her thoughts, or did he communicate to her where he wanted to finally rest? He was ready to go. The vet gave him a sedative before the fatal injection. He died peacefully, his head in Patty's arms.

Animals seem to know when it's time for them to leave this earth. They also understand that death is not something to be feared when your life is complete. The wonderful book *Beyond the Bridge* by Rita Reynolds helped me to understand the wisdom of dying animals. The author found herself in the unsolicited position of providing a home for unwanted animals, many of which were ready to transition. She shared these dying experiences in a loving way that took away much of my pain. It is her belief that animals understand death better than we humans, and will gracefully pass over if their owners don't try to hold them back. Animals have much to teach us about life and death if we will but listen.

My sister Nancy and her family had a wonderful boxer dog, Della. As she got older, Della started to have serious health problems and accompanying pain, although she never complained, just endured. Nancy could be psychic at times and Della would often come to her with a silent plea in her eyes to be released from her suffering life. Nancy knew it was time to allow Della to leave, but her family wasn't ready for life without their beloved dog. Then one day, when Della was together with another livelier dog, Nancy's husband was struck by how old and tired Della looked and he had to admit that she deserved to go.

Della had always entered the veterinarian's office with great trepidation, but on the appointed day she marched right in, went to her prepared space on a soft cushion, fully ready to depart. Her expression said, "thank you, I am at peace," for everyone to see. The whole family was there except for one daughter who, by phone, told Della how much she loved her and would miss her, as the doctor administered the fatal injection. The whole room was in tears. Later, everyone admitted they should have let Della go months before and spared her the suffering she had to endure because of their selfishness in wanting to keep her with them.

When it is time for an animal to be put down, the veterinarian does it so painlessly and easily that the animal doesn't suffer. First they are given a sedative to calm and relax them, then when the injection is administered, it works so quickly that they are gone in about a minute – instantly, it seems. It is we, the ones left behind, who do the suffering, because we know we will miss them so. I can accept euthanasia because it is a release for so many animals that otherwise might have to endure a greatly diminished quality of life, tolerating illness and pain, often without someone to love them the way they deserve. I believe they are then free to roam in the next world, regain healthy robust bodies and possibly reincarnate into a new life as a carefree puppy, kitten, or foal.

Babykins

Each April our local feed store brought in newly hatched baby chickens of assorted varieties. I usually bought five or six of these little fluff balls. Since they needed to be kept warm until they feathered out, I would set them up in the smaller room in the chicken house with a heat lamp, water and baby chick food. They'd huddle tightly together out of fear of the world around them. When I entered the room, in desperation, they'd try to jam themselves through the wall to escape me. Within three weeks they'd have their feathers and the lamp could be removed.

About a month later, the weather would warm enough to open the little door to the outside world. The chicks would not venture out for many days unless I threw them out. A whole new world in their own yard was then available. The senior hens came to the fence to get acquainted, and when the babykins were mature, the two flocks would be merged without disturbance or aggression.

Before we bought our electricity generator, we frequently suffered power outages that could last for hours at a time. On one cold April day, after I had just purchased 20 baby chicks, the power went off, and there was no way to know when it would come back on. The babies would die if I couldn't keep them warm. Even our house was not warm enough for them. Then, I had an inspired flash of genius. I remembered that even in winter, with the windows closed, the interior of my Volvo sitting in the sun was filled with radiant heat. I shooed the chicks into a large box with a little food and water, rushed them to the car, which was, indeed, full of toasty air. The babies were saved.

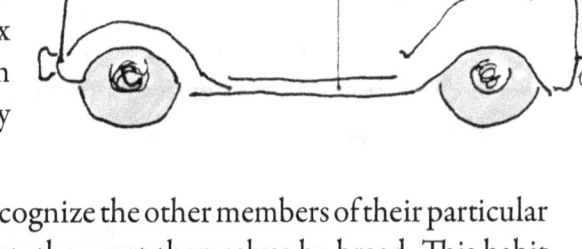

I've observed that chickens seem to recognize the other members of their particular breed. As babies, when they cluster, or rest, they sort themselves by breed. This habit extends into adulthood. If a hen is the only one of her breed, she is usually a bit of a loner, almost an outsider – and chickens are not loners – they need other chickens, as instinct tells them there is protection in groups.

I remembered watching Baby Petunia, a miniature breed, exploring the chicken yard, pecking at various things. She hadn't noticed that all the hens had gone into the henhouse to choose their roosting spots for the night. When she looked up and found she was alone, panic set in. Not knowing what to do, she just stood there, chirping frantically. Inside the henhouse, Mumsy, a mature hen who had just settled herself comfortably on a roosting pole, heard the cries of the frightened one. She jumped down and rushed out to Petunia, who was still standing in the middle of the yard, calling. I saw Mumsy cluck gently to Petunia several times and then lead her into the henhouse. Mumsy was not related to Petunia, but acted out of empathy and compassionate understanding of her plight. Later that evening I went down to the chicken house. Through the window I saw Petunia and Mumsy huddled close together looking out at the moonlit night. The little one was well cared for.

One year I bought five chicks; two Aracanas, two Rhode Island Reds and one Barred Rock. This particular evening, I was in the barn getting ready to feed, when I heard one of the Rhode Islands chirping very loudly and looking about. She was not alone. The Barred Rock was with her, but the other chicks were outside. The sound was one of acute distress. Intuitively, I knew she was missing the other Rhode Island, her sister. I spoke to the disturbed one, who watched me closely and seemed to be listening. I told her that her sister was outside. She stopped chirping, looked me in the eye for a few seconds, stepped to the door and exited to the yard. She spied her sister and ran to her. All was well. Quite honestly, I was very surprised. Apparently, she understood me.

It's a delight to see the little chicks as they discover the world. Anything new, even a dandelion, is considered suspicious and approached with caution. I can almost hear them say to each other, "You try it." "No you go first." "Let's get Mikey, he'll try anything."

Growing up separately, they have no adults to learn from, but instinct has built-in the habits of mature chickens. As wee peeps they know how to do that little hop/scratch to expose hidden seeds. On their first day outside they will find dirt and give themselves a dust bath, just like the big kids.

When they are almost full size, they join the mature chickens. They have gotten acquainted through the fence and won't be attacked as strangers. But they are the new kids, and each has to find her own rank in the pecking order. By six months they start laying and are no longer my babykins.

The Top Cocks

It was late in the afternoon. I was looking for eggs in the nesting/roosting room of the barn when I found Big Red. Red was a magnificent, Aracana rooster. His gold and copper mantle fell over the rust feathers of his back before the iridescent green-black fountain of a tail. Now, his feathers lay wilted, broken and covered with dried sweat. His handsome red comb was caked with blood, dirt, feathers and straw. A bloody stump showed where the second of his grand four-inch spurs had once been.

Red must have been in shock because he did not protest when I picked him up and tucked him under my arm. He wrapped his toes tightly around my fingers, accepting me as his protector. It was obvious what had happened. Harry, the younger rooster, had challenged Red for leadership of the chicken family. Red had lost. His beauty was wilted and he sagged in the shame of defeat.

I carried Red out to the horse trough where I dribbled water over his head to clean off some of his disgrace. Carrying him back to the chicken house, we passed Harry, who stretched himself terribly tall in his pride. He was several years younger than Red; a brash kid just reaching his prime. Harry cockily waggled his head at us with great arrogance. He was the new "top cock" of the barnyard.

Later that evening I went down to the barn to check on Red and found him sitting on the floor facing into the corner of the smaller room. High above him on the roost sat Harry with his harem. In order to give Red a little protection I tilted a board over him like a lean to. In the morning Red was still there, alone, as the hens and Harry had left to get their early morning scratch. Red seemed a bit stronger.

At feeding time that evening I looked for Red, and found him in a corner of the chicken yard by himself. He wore fresh blood and his eyes were swollen almost shut. He barely saw me. Several minutes later I noticed Harry standing over him. Red had moved tightly into the corner with his head tucked under his body. I realized that

Harry had continued his attack through the day and would soon kill Red. That was it! I was really angry with Harry. I threw a stick at him and gave chase, but we both knew I'd never catch him. When we stopped, Harry stretched himself to his tallest and stared back at me with considerable disdain. I had to protect Red. I knew that he needed my care to give him time to recover, or to die in peace. He seemed to want to be alone, so I closed him off in a roosting room with food and water, where Harry couldn't reach him.

Red had always been a gentleman. Whenever he felt I was overstepping my position with the hens he would come up behind me and bump the back of my legs with his body as a gentle warning. He was never aggressive or hostile. I've heard of many other roosters who launched attacks directly at their owners. After Red had battled Old Bob to be king of the hens, he had allowed Bob to live on without harassment, but Harry was a bloody bully.

Since the time Earl rescued Red from drowning in the horse trough, he had been Earl's favorite. Earl had found Red at the point of exhaustion trying desperately to escape from the water, and had scooped up the drowning bird and rushed him to the house. Having lost the strength to struggle further, Red let himself be wrapped in a bath towel. Warm air from my hair dryer saved him from hypothermia and death. After half an hour of sitting on the towel on the bathroom floor he managed to recover his strength and dignity and we returned him to his flock. That incident created a bond between Earl and Big Red. After that whenever Earl called, Red acknowledged him.

The next evening Red was still standing on the floor looking beaten and depressed, as if his life had ended. I picked him up and placed him on a high roosting bar. It was as though I had given him hope. He had a new perspective on the chicken world. He stood up straight, looked around, even preened a few feathers. By morning he almost seemed his old self. But I knew Harry would be eager to continue the fight to the death. I had to make a change.

I'd never paid much attention to Harry until the fight. He had always just been the other rooster in the flock, although I had known that someday he would take over. Red had allowed him rights with the hens so I had expected a showdown would be off in the future. But Harry had earned his right to succeed and he was now "top cock."

Neighbors Ralph and Julie, whose chicken yard adjoined ours, had chickens but no rooster; the perfect place. They were willing to take Red. I was a bit apprehensive as I carried him over to meet his new family. A new chicken is rarely accepted into a flock without adjustment. Perhaps, because he was a rooster, the suspicious hens did not bother him.

Sometime later I looked over and saw Harry and Red trying to continue their fight through the fence that separated the two yards. I'm certain Red realized he could never defeat Harry, but had to stand up for his honor. He probably felt safe with the fence between. I chased Harry off, and fortunately, he did not return. Never again did he go to the fence.

For five days Red stood at the fence gazing back at his lost home and family. It touched me that he might be willing to chance fighting Harry just to be back home. I told a psychic friend about my concern. It was her feeling that Red felt he was being punished, and I should explain to him that I feared for his safety, and that he was to stay in his new home. The whole time I was speaking, he continued to stand at the fence, watching me closely. I felt he was listening. When I was finished I returned to the barn, then looked back. Red was gone. Did he understand what I'd said?

Major Top Hat was one of our bonus roosters. He looked terrific in his shiny, black suit of feathers and huge, brilliant red comb. He had style and considerable self-esteem, which he demonstrated with high steps around the yard. He had just reached maturity and I needed to find him a new home. Marilyn, our neighbor to the south, had just lost a rooster and was willing to take him. I moved him to her yard late one evening.

The Major didn't understand that the move was to be permanent and that he would now have his own harem. The next morning I chanced to look out the window just in time to see Major Top Hat marching across the meadow that separated our yards. He was coming home. Head up, stepping very high he looked like a drum major leading a band. In my head I could even hear the music. I took him back to Marilyn's and, fortunately, this time he stayed.

That fall something happened to Marilyn's chickens, probably dietary, and they lost most of their feathers. Poor Top Hat, a few wilted feathers on his body, and two moth-eaten tail feathers – all he had left – while looking quite ridiculous, he still maintained his poise and held his head high. Happily, his magnificent black suit fully returned.

Six tiny, newly hatched chicks were brought to me in a little cardboard box. I really didn't want them, but to reject them would mean death before their little lives had even started. Since they were miniature I knew they would never produce eggs of sufficient size, and they might have a problem mixing with the larger hens, but I just didn't have the heart to turn them away.

I must admit they were adorable, these wee peeps the size of golf balls. I gave them the smaller hen room where they could develop without harassment from the older chickens. Of mixed silky breeding; one black, a white, two caramel colored, and two in brown, they had fluffy feathered feet, like bedroom slippers.

Almost from the start the smallest one took charge as the leader. Within a very short time he developed the raiment of a beautiful rooster; the golden mantle, iridescent tail and body in rust and brown. Tiny Tim, as I called him, was absolute perfection in miniature, and he thought so too. He was always in full charge of his little flock.

One day I noticed that a caramel girl was having trouble standing. Her legs splayed out from under her, then the white chick developed the same problem. Their conditions worsened. Earl learned that this was a contagious disease from which they would not recover. It was essential that I protect the other hens, so, reluctantly, I released both of them to heaven. The white one got through the fence and was killed by Dakota.

Now there were three Silkies, Tiny Tim and Oliver were roosters, and Bitsy was a girl. Since she was the only female their size they took turns with her. One morning I noticed she was missing, then I discovered her still warm body on the cement floor. A careful examination of her perfect, little form revealed no apparent cause of death. I speculated that she probably knew she would be the joy toy of Tiny Tim and Oliver forever, and decided to leave her body rather than suffer life as their concubine. They then went after the larger hens. When I saw Oliver on the back of a screaming hen, being chased by three other roosters and Tiny Tim, I knew they had to go. As luck would have it, I found that the Humane Society would take chickens, so I took Tiny Tim and Oliver to them.

In twelve years we had many roosters. Each had a distinct personality, but Big Red, Harry and Top Hat were the most memorable of our top cocks. Roosters always have splendid coats, outshining the more subdued hens, and adding a wonderful accent to the chicken yard.

Charles

Four years after Pud and Min had disappeared, Charles joined us. When neighbor Julie said she needed to find a new home for a cat she was caring for that had belonged to her daughter – because he was not getting along with her two cats – I said I'd try him out. Charles, a shorthaired tiger with white chops, bib, tummy, and long white gloves, looked like he was dressed in formal attire.

Julie brought Charles over in an animal carrier. The moment the cage door opened he ran into the bedroom and hid under Earl's bed. To give him time to adjust I put him into the seldom-used morning room with his food, water and bed so he could adjust slowly. I left the door open, and from time to time he would venture out a few feet before rushing back to safety.

Charles had an endearing habit of alternately lifting one paw, then the other like walking in place, curling his toes under and slowly winking his eyes. I believe it might be a trait of cats taken from their mothers at too young an age – a left-over of the kneading habit of kittens. He would also back up to a chair and shiver his tail, reminding me of a tiger in the wild marking his territory. Fortunately, he was fixed and didn't spray urine as they do.

Marshall and Dakota were cautiously introduced to Charles. The dogs didn't cotton to having a new cat about; both thought cats were for chasing. I remembered the time Marshall chased an orange cat, who, in a state of panic, ran straight up a six-foot side of the greenhouse, across a flat roof, then up the gable roof to a spot on top of our two-story garage. I had witnessed this unbelievable feat, and I was also the one who had to get him down, at considerable peril to myself. I didn't wish to repeat the experience. Fortunately, Charles let the two of them know that he wouldn't tolerate nasty dogs.

Our previous cats had been outsiders, while Charles had never been out-of-doors. In order for him to make the transition, I began leaving the door from the living room open to the screen porch. He took to sitting and watching the world from this safe place. Then he discovered the broken screen that Menehuni Mittens had used, and began venturing out into a new world. He tried climbing an apple tree, but fell out, landing on his back, something he never tried a second time.

Spring turned to summer, and my vegetable gardens grew lush and dense. This became Charles's favorite hangout. As many of the plants towered above him, he had his own jungle. The cool, damp earth could feel wonderful on a hot day. He especially liked to lie under the squash plants, which hid him well. Often as I watered, I'd hear his meow, and he'd emerge from under an artichoke plant right next to my feet.

Puddie Pie had been a mouser, Min was adept at catching birds, but Charles took to chasing lizards. When he left one of these beautiful striped creatures as a present in front of the door, I let him know that I wasn't pleased, because these lizards perform a valuable service by eating insects. He didn't leave any more as presents, but I often found dead or dismembered ones about the yard. I guess there is a predator in all cats; except, perhaps, those flat-faced Persian couch potatoes.

We thought he was making a good adjustment, until he started the habit of pulling out his hair in small tufts as he groomed himself. Some days I could find 40 tufts in the middle of the living room floor, 30 tuffs in front of the door, 25 on the bedspread, and probably 14 in Earl's desk chair. I was constantly vacuuming, cleaning, wasting time I couldn't spare. Should I give him back to Julie? The vet said it's often the symptom of anxiety. It was exasperating. If I caught him grooming I would emphatically repeat, "don't pull out your hair." He would stop for a moment and stare at me in confusion, before resuming the hair pulling. Then I learned that, as with children, "don't" statements are confusing; all he heard was "pull" and "hair." I needed to replace my negative statement with a positive one, so I started telling him that he had a very beautiful coat and that he needed to take good care of it. At that point, quite astonishingly, the hair pulling stopped. However, I must admit that being a cat, he only partially cooperated. He stopped hair pulling in the house, but continued the practice on the screen porch.

Charles had another annoying habit – meowing to go out, then, in a short time, meowing to come in again – back and forth. After supper I often sat in a chair beside a window watching TV. Inevitably I'd hear a scratching on the outside of the house behind my head. I'd turn and see a little face and two paws clinging to the windowsill looking at me, and I hear a pathetic meow. When he knew I'd seen him, he'd run around and hop on the wood box on the screen porch. Looking through the glass in the door, he'd stare at me until I let him in. Earl had also seen him stretch for the doorknob in a vain effort to let himself out. I suspected that if he had a companion he might not be so restless. I considered taking a foster cat from the Humane Society, but didn't, out of concern for the multitude of birds that called Wildflower Hill their home.

Sam's Death

Marshall knew before we did that something was wrong with Sam. He would whine, look at Sam, then at me, moving back and forth between us. I just thought he wanted more attention. Then one day, I noticed that Sam was losing weight and drinking a lot of water. She had always been a bit on the plump side, but now I could feel her ribs through her thick, golden coat.

The vet's examination determined that her heart, lungs and stool were normal. He could not feel any tumors. It could be diabetes or cancer. For several hundred dollars the animal hospital could do more testing. The several hundred dollars was a problem. At 12 years, Sam had lived out her life's expectancy. I knew she would never tolerate insulin shots if it was diabetes, and we could never cure cancer.

When Sam and I returned home, I checked all my dog books for guidance. She had stopped eating her dry dog food, picking out and eating only the meat. So, I increased the amount of meat she was getting and added vegetables, which she gobbled up. The book said that dogs should have one third-meat, one-third dry dog food, and one-third vegetables. Vegetables were a new one to me. We often gave the dogs vegetable leftovers, but not regularly. I now cooked up all kinds of vegetables, except onions, which I'd heard could be deadly for dogs. She had always turned her nose up at raw meat, but now relished the raw liver she got. They say that animals know what is best for them, so I trusted her. I gave her nutritional supplements and an Ayurvedic herb used in India for diabetes. Even with lots of TLC she still continued to lose weight and energy. Sam was now bones covered by skin and hair.

By chance a woman came by to look at saddles I had for sale, an animal lover who had studied to be a veterinarian. I discussed Sam and she checked her out. Sam's gums were almost white, an indication that confirmed that she had severe anemia. However, since she wasn't responding to my ministrations, it was clear that the anemia was a symptom of another disease, probably cancer, which is the leading cause of death for dogs.

Sam's decline was swift; about two months from robust health to death. Always a gentle lady of dignity, never once did she moan or cry. I don't know if she was in pain or discomfort, as she never told us in any way. Each day she was slower than the day before. That final week her tail still waved when I spoke to her, but now very slowly.

Marshall drove me crazy; whining, leaning against me or trying to crawl into my lap. He constantly washed Sam's face, cleaned her ears, and checked the scent gland under her tail, which I assumed to be a barometer of health. When Sam stopped eating I knew the end was near. She even turned her head from her favorite dog biscuit "cookie."

Sam had always been an outside dog, but now she stopped using her doghouse, choosing instead to lie upon the ground. Aboriginal peoples say that Mother Earth will transfer healing energy to her creatures if they will lie on Her. Maybe Sam knew this, but I felt that she had already accepted death and was just waiting.

The day we chose to put her down, to spare her unnecessary suffering, was Good Friday. The night before it started to drizzle. I didn't want Sam to sleep her last night out in the rain, so Marshall and I went on a search and finally found her curled up on a nest of dry leaves. I picked her up and carried her into the garage and laid her on rugs with a bowl of water beside her. I told her that we loved her very much and that it was okay to go, if she wanted. I felt she was ready to leave and decided to help her. Marshall was very concerned. Since I didn't want him to disturb her I dragged him out and closed the garage door. As I turned to leave he managed to open the door and rushed back to Sam. Again I dragged him out and this time locked the door. I now believe this was a mistake and that I should have let both dogs take care of themselves and each other. Sam might have been comforted by Marshall's presence, and maybe spending the night outside might have been better for her.

Marshall must have spent the night outside the garage, because in the morning his back was wet from the night long drizzle. Sam could barely stand. I looped a towel under her chest, holding the ends above, forming a sling to assist her in walking. An hour later I put her in the back of Earl's Jeep Cherokee, and Marshall watched from the driveway as we drove off.

Sam had a very sensitive and tender body. I had never been able to move any part of her resting body without a severe warning from her. It had taken years before she was comfortable with even a gentle brushing, as she hated the pull of the brush I worked through her coat. On previous visits to the vet, she had to be muzzled for exams. No one was permitted to poke her body. However, this morning she lay calmly as the vet slipped the lethal needle into her paw. Earl and I held her. Even though we knew Sam was leaving her wasted body for a happy place, we shed many tears. The tears were not for her, but for ourselves and our loss of a wonderful lady.

When we got home I opened the tailgate of the car so Marshall could see Sam didn't return with me. He thoroughly sniffed the spot where he had last seen Sam. Then he was calm and seemed to know she was gone forever. I had anticipated that he would be inconsolable without Sam, as he had spent almost his entire life with her, never apart for more than an hour. But, from that moment his frantic whining stopped. He seemed fine – once again his cheery, loving self. He must have known she was in a better place. However, a couple of days later Earl saw Marshall sitting under the trees where he and Sam had spent so many hours of each day, whimpering softly to himself.

After experiencing several deaths of beloved animals, in trying to protect them I had moved them from where they had chosen to be into places I thought were better for them. Separating them from their beloved companions, I may have increased their pain. I would in the future allow them to choose the circumstances for their death.

Dakota

After Samantha Josephine died, we wanted to get another dog as a companion for Marshall. The two of them had been so close, I was sure Marsh would be devastated by her death, but, surprisingly, he wasn't. I believe he knew she was dying and, possibly, accepted her going as her choice. Still, we desired another dog.

Earl wanted a Lab puppy, but I wanted another breed, a mature dog. The Humane Society told me about their foster program – a good way to try a dog before committing to the purchase. After several trips to the Humane Society I saw Dakota, who looked a lot like Sam. A two-year-old Australian Shepherd/Collie mix, her same size and build, with the same double coat, except that his was brown with a black dusting on top, rather than the golden color hers had been. The society asked if I would like to foster him and his companion Coco. Since Dakota and Coco had grown up together, I took them both home.

They immediately loved Wildflower Hill, and side-by-side they explored every corner of our two-acre yard. Coco was fascinated by the chickens which, fortunately, were well protected by a high fence. They had great fun chasing the cat, Charles. But, when they jointly showed aggression toward Marshall I decided one must go.

I hated to separate them, but Coco had to leave. It broke my heart to have to drag her into my car, whining and crying. Later the Humane Society told me that alone in her cell, without Dakota, she whined pathetically. I hoped she would find her own family.

From the start Dakota attached himself to me like glue. I understood that he felt he, too, might be returned. Whenever I was outside he was there immediately. When I went indoors he circled the house watching for me to come out. I always left my shoes outside the door when I entered the house, and after Dakota learned that I would exit where my shoes were, that's where he waited. If I didn't enter the house immediately after giving him his food he would leave the food to follow me. That necessitated changing mealtime from morning to evening, placing his food bowl beside the door as I went in to my supper.

When Sam was dying I had desperately consulted all my animal books, looking for any remedies that might help her. As one book said it was important for dogs to have about a third of their food as vegetables, I immediately began adding squash, carrots, broccoli, cabbage and such to their food. At first, Dakota wouldn't touch this strange food and Marshall would always clean up his veggies. Since Marshall loved vegetables Dakota decided they must be O.K. and started eating them. That summer Marsh took to eating raw carrots and even apples as they ripened and fell from the trees. In the fall both dogs would help themselves to grapes, picking them right off the vine.

Dakota was a free spirit with a sometimes-primitive streak, often demonstrating wolf-like characteristics, the best and the worst. He was full of love and affection for humans but very capable of looking after his interests and defending his territory against dogs.

I had taken Dakota as a foster child and I almost took him back. The first time I brushed him, Marshall, wanting to be brushed also, kept pressing his body to mine. I yelled at him to "git." He turned to settle under a nearby pine tree. Immediately, Dakota rushed from me, leapt on Marshall, growling, snarling tearing at the back of his neck. I screamed at him and managed to pull him off Marshall, who had never been attacked by anything in his life, was shocked by this aggression, as all he had ever known was love. I comforted him and tended his bleeding head and ear.

Dakota was chained up for the rest of the day. He whined, barked and pulled at the chain. When I released him we had a long talk and I explained that I would not tolerate him attacking Marshall. If he didn't behave I would take him back to the Humane Society. He profusely begged my forgiveness; whining, pawing me, full of kisses. I understood that he was very jealous of Marshall and knew he was full of anxiety, and feared I wouldn't keep him. But, he must abide by the rules of good behavior.

Several days later he again attacked Marshall. This time no blood. Again, he was chained up for several hours, protesting the entire time. Another talk. Finally, he seemed to understand that Marshall belonged on the ranch, and that bad behavior wouldn't be tolerated. However, Dakota usually forced his way between us when I was petting Marshall. And, when we walked Dakota pressed his body against my legs, trying to be very close.

Marshall was amazing. This wonderful animal with the great and loving heart, always forgave Dakota. However, when Dakota got a bit rambunctious, Marshall cautiously kept a wary eye on him. Most of the time Dakota demonstrated warm affection for Marsh, blessing him with kisses and challenging him to playtime. I was very careful not to favor Marshall with too much attention, to avoid Dakota's jealousy. Seldom could I play Marshall's favorite ball chasing game if Dakota was near. No longer could Marshall even try to chase it because Dakota will beat him out, never picking up the ball, just beating out Marsh and taking possession. If I restrained Dakota so Marsh could fetch, on Marshall's return, Dakota would snap at him. Whenever Dakota was off somewhere, I'd give Marshall some special attention of his own, both of us keeping an eye out for Dakota, who would rush in and usurp Marshall's TLC time. Marshall would keep looking over his shoulder afraid that Dakota would arrive at any moment.

It seemed that Dakota was trying to dominate me, Marshall, and the other animals. I had unwittingly rewarded this behavior by giving him additional attention. Now I needed to let him know that I was the leader. I would pet him only when I wanted to, not whenever he wanted it. It was important that he learn to sit, and down on my command. Whenever he tried to control other animals I would distract him and break that focus. He learned very quickly, and within a week our problems seemed to disappear. I now understood where he was coming from, and anticipated that from then on I would be able to handle any eventuality, and that he would be a wonderful friend for many years to come.

Dakota's behavior toward people was as loving and demonstrative as you could ever want. Visitors always received welcoming wags and kisses. Marshall's love was more reserved; no kisses from him. Even though he loved people Dakota was a good watchdog, always alerting us to what was happening, but not like our obnoxious neighbor dogs, who barked wildly at any excuse. We'd hear gentle woofs from Dakota, unless he determined it was something serious and we might be threatened. When he issued his warning about an intruder, he kept an eye on the house, watching for me to respond.

When Earl told me that Dakota sometimes waited all day by the gate, watching every car that went by, it made me very sad. At times he would dig out, run down our long drive to wait for my return in the middle of the street. I decided to tell him that I planned to return and give him a time. That seemed to work and he no longer devoted his days to waiting for me.

Whenever we were apart for a couple of hours, Dakota couldn't contain himself with excitement upon my return. In the evening when I drove to the gate, Dakota would hardly let me get it open as he overwhelmed me with his welcome, expressing his excitement with high squeaky sounds. Then he'd dash off to tell Marshall I was home, running in circles, wagging his tail and smiling broadly. I was his life, the center of his world. He would allow me to leave in my car, however, if I went off in someone else's car he became desperate, thinking, perhaps, I was being abducted and wouldn't be back. When the horses were out browsing the yard, Dakota often followed them around, continually looking back at me. I realized he was looking to me for instruction. As I called the horses for dinner, Dakota would start driving them, nipping at their heels and flanks, usually running them to the far corner of the property. His shepherd blood was trying to tell him something that confused him. I needed to learn how to teach him the work he was bred for as a herding dog, but I didn't know how to begin.

One of Dakota's most endearing traits was his singing. Usually about seven or eight o'clock in the evening he'd start, his voice swinging up in a high, clear howl only to descend and fall apart in a cracking way, a few nips and personal touches to end, sounding like a wind-up toy unwinding. Samantha Josephine used to so delight me with her singing and now Dakota sang the same songs that I loved so much.

Although both Dakota and Marshall had doghouses, Dakota, like Sam, preferred to sleep out under the stars. Marshall loved his house, but as he got older I didn't want him to suffer the cold. When the nights got down in the teens I started letting him sleep in the garage next to the furnace. Since he had never needed to be house broken I wasn't certain he would control himself in the garage. That first night just before I retired I decided to take him out. I entered the garage called him saying, "O.K. Marshall, let's go pee-pee." It amazed me that he knew exactly what I was saying. I can report that he never had an accident in the garage.

Dakota killed a chicken, chased the cat, attacked Marshall and tried to nip the horses. I seriously considered taking him back to the Humane Society, but I knew he probably wouldn't survive being without me. He was so loving and devoted to me that I always forgave him. I knew there was hope, and that we could make progress in teaching him how to be a mature companion.

Goodbye Darlin' Keebe

Nina and I had just celebrated Poco's 29th birthday, and I was looking two months ahead to a party for Keebe's 29th birthday. I had just come home from work and noticed that Keebe was half down, head up with legs tucked under her body. She called to me in a loud distressed voice. Poco echoed the call. I was concerned, as she never lies down late in the day. As I rushed to her, she lay out flat. I talked to her quietly, asking what was wrong. She had a couple of cuts on her body, but I couldn't tell what had happened. I ran toward the house to call her veterinarian, and looking back I saw her struggle to her feet, and on very shaky legs move to Poco's yard.

The vet said he could come immediately, so I rushed back to the corral. Keebe was down again next to the fence. I spoke to her and told her the doctor was coming, and that he would help her feel better. She lay quietly, but I could tell she was in pain. On the phone the vet surmised it was colic. When she got up, we walked around the yard trying to relieve her stress.

Doctor Killian arrived quite promptly. He looked at her gums, which were pale, her pulse and heart rate were rapid. He was very worried. All he knew to do was treat her for colic, which necessitated giving her mineral oil through a tube in her nose. In an attempt to force the tube up her nostril, he ruptured the membranes and the blood poured out. As he left the shelter through the barn to get more sedative, Keebe called after him through the open door. I had told her he would help her, and I felt her call to him was saying that he should come back, that he hadn't helped her yet. After administering more sedative he succeeded in getting the tube up the other nostril. A gallon of mineral oil was pumped into her stomach and the tube withdrawn. With nostrils flared she was breathing heavily, shaking unsteadily.

A gentle rain started. I was reminded of the drizzle the night Samantha Josephine died. The vet wanted Keebe to stay warm and dry. She had the habit of standing out in the rain, so I tied a rope across the entrance to the shelter. I blanketed her even though she was sweating a cold sweat. I told her that I loved her very much, that I wanted her to live, but if she wanted to go, it was all right. And, I prayed. Later that night I went down to check on her. Her condition was the same. I prayed some more.

In the morning, with great apprehension, I started down toward the shelter. I could see four, white legs on the ground projecting into view just past the stall opening. I feared the worse. Going through the barn to the shelter I saw her stretched out in the mud. Keebe had broken the rope that had held her in. I saw that her legs were stiff and raised off the ground. She had gone. There was no life in her body.

Poco had spent the night in Keebe's shelter, as she was in his. I felt she would be more comfortable his larger space. I now let him join her. He rushed to her side and gently touched her body with his lips; first her shoulder, then her back, her flank, and several times her eye, trying to wake her from her deep sleep. He repeated this throughout the day, standing by her side.

The next morning, Valentine's Day, a huge backhoe arrived to dig her grave. When the six-foot deep hole was finished, the backhoe bucket picked up Keebe's body and carried her to the site. At this point Poco, who had been calm, began running around the backhoe, calling in distress. After her body was dropped into the hole and covered, Poco became even more agitated. I told him that Keebe was gone, and that we would soon find a new friend for him.

Nina came out each day to work with him; talking to him, bringing him treats, lots of touching and massage. It seemed to help to ease his hurt. I, too, gave him extra attention. We were told that it is important to maintain a horse's usual routine at times like these. Mealtimes were the hardest for Poco. They had always been fed together, so he looked for Keebe and called for her. I repeatedly told him he would soon have a new friend. Horses are herd animals, and it is stressful for them to be alone.

Keebe had been a delightful friend, and a joy to watch. Everyone who knew her loved her. Probably her only fault was eating peaches and apples off the trees, but she always stopped when I yelled at her. Now I'd let her eat as many peaches as she wanted, if I could only have her back. Keebe was my great treasure, my princess, an ongoing delight, bringing me much joy – everything I ever wanted in a horse – always there with a warm greeting, always willing to do whatever I ask, always bringing a smile to my heart. And, Poco loved her dearly, too. I hoped she had been happy with us. I believe she was.

Rainbow

Keebe's death left Poco as the only horse, so we needed to find a new companion for him as soon as possible. Once again I put up a card on the feed store bulletin board. Laurie, a college student, responded, and a day later she brought her horse Faith, a retired race horse. The grooms at the track, instead of leading her around by a halter found it was quicker and easier to just to grab an ear and pull her around. Of course, this was exceedingly painful to Faith, and she would no longer allow anyone to touch her head, so Laurie had to lead her about by a loose rope around her neck. This can be a problem when you need to control a thousand pounds of horse.

Mostly, Faith just stayed in her corral. When Poco was allowed out to munch about the ranch she just watched with yearning, because she was not allowed out without a halter, as I might not be able to get her back to the corral. She let me know she was upset. I then indicated to her that if she allowed the halter she would be able to graze outside, too. I would stand at the gate holding the halter. Finally, she decided the halter was a reasonable price for nibbling green grass about the yard. After that I never had a problem putting a halter on her. Of course, I always did it very gently without touching her ears so as not to upset her.

Faith wasn't with us too long because Laurie never paid her food and stabling bills. After four months that was enough.

Once again, I was on the lookout for another horse to roommate with the one still with me.

Someone told me about a woman, Jo, who had an Arab gelding she wasn't using and would permit me to keep and ride, if I were willing to feed and board him. I went to check out Rainbow, who was sharing a pen with a much larger horse, who was obviously the boss. Here was a rather undistinguished, white Arabian with a thin, scraggly mane and a short, wispy, pathetic tail who held his head low. By nature, Arabian horses are quite proud of their distinguished blood, and possess luxurious manes and tails, but not Rainbow. He looked very sad and beaten down, but here was a horse I didn't have to buy, that I could ride. I'd take him.

The next day Jo trailered Rainbow over. He was very well mannered and I noticed he was easy to handle as she led him into his stall. Jo told me that the next day she would be back to pick him up and take him for a vet appointment to have his teeth floated.

Later that evening, I went down to check if he was comfortable and found him out in the yard munching grass. I was quite startled and said out loud, "Bow, what are you doing out here? You're supposed to be in your stall." His head immediately popped up, he looked at me, and imagine my amazement when in my head I heard him say, "I just wanted to look around." I turned and picked up a lead rope and headed toward him. He started quickly to move away. I then heard him say, "Put down the rope, open the door and I will put myself back." I knew that if I continued to move toward him he would easily outrun me and I might spend the evening trying fruitlessly to catch him. So, I did as he asked, put down the rope and opened the stall door. He promptly did as he said he would do, returning to his stall. I had become accustomed to talking to my animals, but this was the first time I heard one speak back to me.

The next morning as I gave him his feed, I told him that Jo would be coming to pick him up for his appointment to get his teeth floated, which all horses hate. Apparently, he understood what I said, because this usually very cooperative horse decided he wouldn't go. Jo and her husband arrived and she entered the corral with his halter, expecting him to come to her. Rainbow took off running around his large yard and would have nothing to do with her. That game could go on for hours. I knew we would have to trick him, so I got Poco and led him through the corral to graze in the yard. Jo stood by the gate. Bow thought he might get to go out, too, if he submitted to Jo and the halter. That did it. She got him and he was off to the veterinarian.

I soon learned that this amazing animal understood what I said. He had a reoccurring problem with an eye that periodically watered, for which the vet had prescribed a salve, that Jo said he resisted. Since I didn't like to use prescription drugs, preferring to use natural ways, I created a natural remedy. It was a very watery solution, and horses don't like water on their faces. I talked directly to Bow telling him I needed to tend to his eye and he must stand still. He listened, and as I sloshed the solution on his eye and it ran down his face, he stood very still. And, my remedy worked.

Poco and Bow got along well, glad for each others' company. Bow's spirits improved and he seemed to be happy. He held his head high, was alert and responsive, no longer the downtrodden creature I first met. With jubilance he would sometimes trot around his corral like a show horse; head raised, ears alert, tail up like a flag, his long legs stepping high. Whenever I saw this display I would clap my hands and shout encouragement, telling him how beautiful he was, and he loved it. Round and round, stepping higher and looking radiant, he was in his glory. I could feel him glowing with happiness.

Bow had a good heart and never misbehaved, but he did like to tease me on occasion. Our neighbor had an overgrown pasture and I had permission for the horses to go over for munch time. I would lead them over and turn them loose. It had never occurred to Poco to ever be uncooperative, but one day Bow decided he didn't want to come home and when I tried to collect him he gleefully ran off. I could see him smiling with delight as he played his little game. After repeated attempts to get him I realized that could go on for some time. I also knew if I took Poco home Bow would then want to come too. As I led Poco off Bow called me back to get him.

We had been through this routine several times, Poco following without a lead attached to his halter as he never wanted to be left behind. One day as I led Bow to the gate and opened it Bow stopped. In my mind I heard him say, "I know what to do, let go of the rope and I will go in myself." As he requested, I let him go and he took himself to his corral at the far end of the property, never stopping to munch along the way as horses usually try to do. Bow always honored what he said.

Bow was highly intelligent and at times when he became bored, could find some mischief. The horse trough was a retired bath tub next to a faucet with a hose connecting the two. Sometimes Bow would pick up the hose in his mouth and wave it about, and several times he managed to pull the plug in the tub, draining the water. But then he would turn on the water, trying to refill the tub. I was able to correct this naughty behavior when I carefully explained the problem and the repercussions to him.

Living at Wildflower Hill transformed Bow into a beautiful Rainbow, as his naturally joyful nature was freed and life was stimulating. He was loved and honored, he had a large yard all to himself, a nice companion, Poco, in an adjoining corral. He was talked to, allowed to graze on green grass in different areas, and he was ridden on interesting excursions around the neighborhood. What more could he have wanted?

After several months, the morning arrived when I found Poco lying on the ground. He had departed his body in favor of a new home in heaven. It was unexpected and very hard for Nina, as well as for me. Once again I found myself with one horse. Bow didn't seem to be overly distressed, but content to be on his own with me. By now Earl had passed from heart disease and his son had died of diabetes and celiac disease. Life on the ranch was winding down. I decided not to get another horse. I had become very attached to Bow and was reluctant to send him back to his owner, as he had become more like a human friend than an animal. However, since I had decided it was also time for me to leave the ranch, it was time to send Bow home to Jo.

A short time later I went over to Jo's to visit Bow. I hardly recognized him. Once again he was spending his days standing in the pen with the bully horse. His joyful nature had once again descended into depressed submission. Bow would not acknowledge or even look at me. He looked sad and, again, was carrying his head low. I believe he could not forgive me for taking away his happy life and returning him to the unhappy life he had escaped from with me. I felt devastated that he was no longer the glorious Arabian horse I knew he was in his heart.

Wrap

Earl and E.J., Cindy, Keebe, Poco, Samantha Josephine, Menehuni Mittens and Puddie Pie had all died. Rainbow had returned to his owner. Because the horses were gone, the chickens now had no protectors from coyotes, and after several raids there were few left. It was devastating to view the slaughtered bodies left by the coyotes. I confined the remaining girls to the henhouse and their small yard with the high fence, telling them they must not fly over, that if they stayed in the small yard they would be safe. None flew over, as they feared the fate of the other hens. Fortunately, I found someone who wanted my girls, and they were taken away to a new home.

What an amazing collection of personalities we enjoyed in the multitude of animals that lived with us, each one a unique individual. I treasure the memory of the dove couple who trustingly built a nest in the window-box outside our kitchen window. They watched us as we moved about the kitchen, sometimes as close as three feet. So many lovely, sweet doves lived with us most of the year, coming to accept that we cared about them. They'd stroll, as doves do, around the yard accepting that they lived in a place of peace.

Twenty years had passed at Wildflower Hill, I was older than when we started, and now alone. The burden of caring for the property by myself was overwhelming and I knew the work was beginning to take a great toll on me physically. No longer did I need to grow the great abundance of food we had once enjoyed. I decided it was time for me to leave, also. I had earned the right to a comfortable retirement.

Fortunately, the Vargas, new neighbors next door, wanted to buy the property. They loved Dakota and Charles so they could stay in their home. Marshall was by now going on 15, well over 100 in human years, and his joints had become stiff, so that he found it difficult to move freely. His breathing was quite heavy and noisy. The new owners didn't want him and since I was moving to a rented condo, the only thing to do was to put him down. It was a painful decision, but I knew that when he passed over he would again have a young, energetic body and be able to play his favorite game of ball, and he would be with Sam, Earl, and E.J., the ones he loved so dearly.

There is a dog in my new neighborhood in California, Tanner, who looks just like Marshall as he was when I last saw him; the same happy, friendly personality, waving tail, stiff joints and raspy breathing. Tanner warms my heart whenever I see him, remembering Marshall Goodboy.

Life at Wildflower had come to an end. What wonderful memories I have of all the fantastic kids we shared our lives with; the births, the deaths, the pain, the joy. All are treasured memories that I have recorded in this book to share with others who understand the great joy animals can bring into our lives.

We can learn so much about life from our animal friends. Here is a code for living from a dog that can enrich our lives and our world.

- When loved ones come home, always run to greet them.
- Thrive on attention and let people touch you.
- When you're happy, dance around and wag your entire body.
- If what you want lies buried, dig until you find it.
- Avoid biting when a single growl will do.
- Run, romp and play daily.
- On hot days, drink lots of water and lie under a shady tree.
- On warm days, stop to lie on your back in the grass.
- Be loyal.
- Eat with gusto and enthusiasm. Stop when you've had enough.
- Delight in the joy of a long walk.
- Never pretend to be something you're not.
- When someone is having a bad day, be silent, close by and gently nuzzle them.
- Be always grateful for each new day.

– Unknown